INSTRUCTIONS FOR POLITICIANS

The Best of Edmund Burke

Introduced and edited by Gary Furnell

Foreword by Hon. Kevin Andrews

I0631892

Connor Court Publishing

Published in 2024 by Connor Court Publishing Pty Ltd.

Connor Court Publishing Pty Ltd
PO Box 7257
Redland Bay QLD 4165
sales@connorcourt.com
www.connorcourt.com
Phone 0497-900-685

Printed and bound in Australia.

ISBN: 9781923224117

Cover design: Tim Jones.
Cover images: John Constable, Salisbury Cathedral from the Bishop's Garden, 1826, oil on canvas, 88.9 x 112.4 cm (Frick Collection, New York).
The tragic end of Marie Antoinette, anonymous artist, 1793, via the British Museum.

The Philosophical Notes

No. 3

Previous Volumes

No.1

The Evolution of Evolution by St. George Jackson Mivart

No.2

That Which is Seen and That Which is Not Seen

together with *What is Government?* and

Petition of the Candlemakers

by Frédéric Bastiat

CONTENTS

FOREWORD

Edmund Burke was born in 1729 and died in 1797. He spent 28 years (December 1765 - July 1794) in the House of Commons, yet the highest political office he achieved was Paymaster of the Forces, a role he occupied for just a few months. Despite this modest achievement, Burke remains one of the towering political figures of his era. His writings remain as pertinent today as when they were published. His influence on conservatism has been profound. As Russell Kirk wrote in *The Conservative Mind*, "Burke is the founder of our conservatism."

Following his election as the Member for Bristol in 1774, Burke addressed constituents on his role as their member. His response was both courageous and clear. The question he responded to is still asked of members of parliament, partly because of the designation 'representative'.

Many years ago, I received a letter from a constituent demanding that I vote in a particular manner as his 'representative'. A few days later, I received a similar letter demanding that I vote in the opposite manner, again as the 'representative' of the second constituent. While there are a range of constituent views about every matter before the Parliament, this was the only time that I had received almost identical letters explicitly demanding that I vote in two contrary ways as the 'representative' of each of the constituents. Each writer pressed me to 're-present' their views. I wrote a similar response to each person, indicating that I had received the two letters demanding that I 're-present' the view of each of them in my vote, but asking how could I do so. I never received a reply.

Another version of this approach is to demand that a Representative vote according to the will of a majority of constituents. But views often change, and it is almost impossible to discern the attitude of the majority on any issue. Bills are amended and changed. Times don't allow ongoing consultations. The only occasion in three decades that I had a clear indication of the views of my constituents was on the marriage debate when a plebiscite was conducted. Even then, many constituents didn't vote.

More significantly, the 'representative' approach confuses the role of the member of parliament, as Burke powerfully stated in 1774.

> It ought to be the happiness and glory of a representative to live in the strictest union, the closest correspondence, and the most unreserved communication with his constituents. Their wishes ought to have great weight with him; their opinion, high respect; their business, unremitted attention. It is his duty to sacrifice his repose, his pleasures, his satisfactions, to theirs; and above all, ever, and in all cases, to prefer their interest to his own. But his unbiassed opinion, his mature judgment, his enlightened conscience, he ought not to sacrifice to you, to any man, or to any set of men living. These he does not derive from your pleasure; no, nor from the law and the constitution. They are a trust from Providence, for the abuse of which he is deeply answerable. Your representative owes you, not his industry only, but his judgment; and he betrays, instead of serving you, if he sacrifices it to your opinion.
>
> My worthy colleague says, his will ought to be subservient to yours. If that be all, the thing is innocent. If government were a matter of will upon any side, yours, without question, ought to be

superior. But government and legislation are matters of reason and judgment, and not of inclination; and what sort of reason is that, in which the determination precedes the discussion; in which one set of men deliberate, and another decide; and where those who form the conclusion are perhaps three hundred miles distant from those who hear the arguments?

To deliver an opinion, is the right of all men; that of constituents is a weighty and respectable opinion, which a representative ought always to rejoice to hear; and which he ought always most seriously to consider. But *authoritative* instructions; *mandates* issued, which the member is bound blindly and implicitly to obey, to vote, and to argue for, though contrary to the clearest conviction of his judgment and conscience, - these are things utterly unknown to the laws of this land, and which arise from a fundamental mistake of the whole order and tenor of our constitution.

Parliament is not a *congress* of ambassadors from different and hostile interests; which interests each must maintain, as an agent and advocate, against other agents and advocates; but parliament is a *deliberative* assembly of *one* nation, with *one* interest, that of the whole; where, not local purposes, not local prejudices, ought to guide, but the general good, resulting from the general reason of the whole. You choose a member indeed; but when you have chosen him, he is not the member of Bristol, but he is a member of *parliament*. If the local constituent should have an interest, or should form an hasty opinion, evidently opposite to the real good of the rest of the community, the member for that place ought to be as far, as any other, from any endeavour to give it effect.

Albeit one, relatively short speech, Burke's response to the merchants of Bristol contains a number of the principles of conservatism while recognising that the philosophy is protean rather than dogmatic. The first is the belief in providence, along with individual conscience.

Flowing from this is a recognition of wise judgment and the rejection of prescriptions from any individuals, especially those with abstract ideas for progress. Other principles of conservatism were developed in various speeches and writings.

For contemporary parliamentarians and policymakers, three aspects of Burke are pertinent. These are his discussions about the intergenerational nature of society; the so-called 'little platoons'; and, by implication, the limits of government and the dangers of the political sphere dominating all others. These are the inter-related pillars of modern conservatism.

A compact between generations

It flows from the belief that prudential judgements rather than hasty adherence to the latest thoughts or new trends, a valuing of the existing while being open to change, and the existence of enduring values that Burke would recognise a compact across generations. As he stated:

> Society is indeed a contract.....[But, a]s the ends of such a partnership cannot be obtained in many generations, it becomes a partnership not only between those who are living, but between those who are living, those who are dead, and those who are to be born. Each contract of each particular state is but a clause in the great primaeval contract of eternal society. . . Changing the state as often as there are floating fancies...no one generation could link with the other. Men would be little better than the flies of a summer.

A compact between generations demands prudential judgments. Many policy-makers pursue their desired, intended outcomes, but neglect the unintended and undesired. Considering the impact of proposed actions over generations, not months or years, brings additional factors to the decision-making process. An intergenerational compact also reinforces the long-term good of the whole of society.

Little platoons

Although the expression 'little platoons' seems dated, the notion of small groups of connected individuals remains the essential basis of a well-functioning society. It is at this local, practical and familiar level that individuals gain meaning in their lives. It also forms the basis of the nation.

> To be attached to the subdivision, to love the little platoon we belong to in society, is the first principle (the germ as it were) of public affections. It is the first link in the series by which we proceed towards a love to our country and to mankind.

These are the groups - family, church and local communities - that orient men and women toward virtues such as temperance and fortitude.

The modern state is relentless in substituting other structures for these basic institutions, questioning their competence, doubting their usefulness and even suggesting that they fail individuals.

Burke's insistence on their centrality to society was not only practical; he maintained that these groups educated individuals in the necessary virtues for both personal and societal benefit. Such groups anchor individuals in society. They counter the abstract – and the tendency, too prevalent – of the dissolution of nations into mere aggregations of individuals.

It is the habits, dispositions and culture of people that undergird democracy. As Jean Bethke Elshtain has written: "Democracy is not simply a set of procedures or a constitution, but an ethos, a spirit, a way of responding, and a way of conducting oneself."

Consequently, a state without public discussion and civil association lacks a democratic life-force. As Alexis de Tocqueville observed almost 200 years ago, it is the association of people in a myriad of groups and organisations that underpins the modern democratic experiment.

This 'little platoons' web of associations to which we belong, has become known as civil society. They are the relationships and institutions that are neither created nor controlled by the state. "The essential task of civil society – families, neighbourhood life, and the web of religious, economic, educational, and civic associations – is to foster competence and character in individuals, build social trust, and help children become good people and good citizens." Hence democracy is built upon the virtues of personal and civic responsibility.

The notion is not new. Adam Smith in *The Theory of Moral Sentiments* posited the centrality of ethical values, including care for others, as a necessary basis of the market system. In his observations of the new American republic, Alexis de Tocqueville noted:

> Among the laws that rule human societies, there is one which seems to me more precise and clear than all others. If men are to remain civilised or to become so, the art of associating together must grow and improve in the same ratio in which equality of conditions is increased.

It is this sense of mutual association that Tocqueville observed in America that stands at the heart of a well-functioning democratic nation. It is not a new notion.

It has been unfashionable to speak about virtues for a long time. But this is at variance with most of civilised history.

This notion of virtue is missing from our modern discussion. As Lord Hailsham has said:

> Virtue must be an intrinsic interest of secular society and a society which does not seek to identify what types of conduct are intrinsically virtuous and to support and encourage them as a matter of policy and to discourage their opposites would itself be neither rational nor capable of enjoining that cohesion without which stable and civilised society cannot exist.

The central core of conservatism - the unifying principle upon which other categories and manifestations rest – is the recognition and support of these institutions. As Yuval Levin put it:

> The premise of conservatism has always been that what matters most about society happens in the space between the individual and the state - the space occupied by families, communities, civic and religious institutions, and the private economy - and that sustaining, relating and protecting that space and helping all ... take part in what happens there are among the foremost purposes of government.

Rather than viewing these mediating institutions with suspicion, conservatives believe they are critical to a well-functioning society. Government should not seek to usurp their function and role, but allow them to operate as separate spheres of activity.

The limits of government

The belief that government should be limited is not unique to conservatism; it is an idea shared with classic liberals. It is one reason that conservatives and classic liberals have been capable of working together in government in various places, particularly in Australia.

13

Burke's expression of the limitation is manifest in his *Reflections*. It is central to his criticism of Rousseau and others, albeit expressed differently. When the state dominates, all becomes political and the tendency towards totalitarianism manifests itself. As the experience of Covid demonstrates, this tendency, if unchecked, can destroy freedoms and liberties. Even corporations have allowed themselves to become instruments of the state in the pursuit of the *zeitgeist*.

Conclusion

Burke's writings are as relevant today as they were in the 18th century. The incursion of the state into other spheres of activity has been unrelenting. Understanding - and endeavouring to apply - Burke's thought to contemporary public policy issues is as critical today.

The value of this collection is that it goes to the heart of Burke's thought, while sparing the reader what is often viewed as flowery language of the 18th century.

Many MPs know little of their political philosophy beyond superficial statements such as "I support freedom of speech". Gary Furnell has provided a useful resource in collecting together the most valuable thoughts and writings of Edmund Burke in this volume. It deserves a wide readership.

KEVIN ANDREWS, Member of Australian House of Representatives, 1991-2022.

INTRODUCTION

Edmund Burke (1729-1797) was an Irishman, born in Dublin, who lived in England from his youth until his death. He had a Catholic background and strong Catholic sympathies, but Burke was raised Anglican, a shrewd move by his father because it meant Edmund escaped the educational and career restrictions imposed on Catholics in England. He studied at Trinity College and after graduating moved to London. He aspired to a law career, but abandoned this profession, angering his father who cut off Edmund's allowance. During this time of penury in his mid-twenties, Edmund read prodigiously and started to write with some success.

Towards the end of this period, he married. He wrote about his bride, Jane:

> 'Tis the sweetness of Temper, Benevolence, Innocence, and Sensibility which a face can express, that forms her beauty ... Her eyes have a mild light, but they awe you when she pleases; they command, not like a good man out of office, but by virtue. Her Stature is not tall. She is not made to be the admiration of everyone, but the happiness of one. She has all the delicacy that does not exclude firmness. Her smiles are—inexpressible...

His beloved wife followed Edmund's Anglican attendance. Their quiet but steady religious adherence was important to the couple.

Burke's first book was a treatise on the sublime and the beautiful; it brought him public attention. He gained employment as secretary to a variety of politicians, one of whom, the Marquis of Rockingham, became Prime Minister. Burke's political connections helped him, aged 35, to gain a seat in Parliament. Burke's strong Irish, Catholic and colonial sympathies made him—while not quite an outsider—a somewhat unusual figure in English politics.

His political opponents and even some of his colleagues sniffed at his large Irish family; he was always welcoming more—and more needy kin—into his household's ambit. Overall, Edmund and Jane's marriage and family life were happy. But not every instance of family fondness and proximity was prudent. Edmund was repeatedly criticised for his association with his brother Richard and cousin William. They pursued shady financial dealings at a time when Edmund was criticising corrupt politicians. In later years, he tried but failed to gain for his son Richard a well-paid position in the Exchequer. At the same time Edmund's party, the Whigs, were promoting bills in Parliament to suppress jobbing and cronyism.

It was perhaps for quite minor but public misjudgements like these that he was never elevated to Cabinet. But he was given an important position: Paymaster of the Forces. The appointment wasn't long, but he gained an intimate knowledge of government finances. It's likely the shrewdest of his colleagues recognised that his greatest service was to articulate with memorable eloquence and persuasive impact what had hitherto been inchoate and obscure: the instinctive, cautious political empiricism of the English people. He gave voice to these sound instincts in principles which were built on firm faith in the wisdom of God and the slowly accumulative practical goodness of common people. But it took crises to stir Burke to this enduring work.

Burke was a parliamentarian from 1765 to 1794. At first, he was the member for Wendover, later he was the Member for Bristol. In 1780 he lost this hotly contested seat and afterwards became the member for Malton. Parliament, during these years, was quiet at first but soon faced alarms and revolutions. In the early 1770s, Burke supported the American colonials' claims for greater autonomy. Initially, the colonials were not seeking a complete break with England. They were devout, orderly people, not philosophical radicals who wanted to remake their societies—discarding all that had been achieved—to implement speculative social theories. Burke warned Parliament that punitive taxes and recalcitrant policies would antagonise the sturdy, industrious Americans. The English were governing *against* the people, not *for* them; it was (and still is) a sure means of stirring resentment and rebellion. His warnings didn't win sufficient favour to change policies, although England's potential risks were immense. The American War of Independence began. England lost the war and her New England colonies. The United States of America was born.

In contrast, Burke was aghast at the French revolution. It was entirely different to the American Revolution, although the French *philosophes* drew inspiration from the American colonists' struggle. The French revolutionaries based their ideas not on political and social realities but on abstract notions, in particular the elevated ideals of Liberty, Fraternity and Equality. The would-be leaders of this revolutionary fervour were not practical men. They weren't orderly, neighbourly or devout. They didn't value sufficiently their country's heritage, seeing only the manifest wrongs and not the less obvious but still valuable qualities of the French kingdom. They demanded a fresh start, a clean slate for a new society and this meant the destruction of existing social classes, privileges and customs, together with the erasure of local loyalties, chivalrous manners and religious bonds. In short, everything that characterised the *Ancien Regime*.

Burke often visited France and had grown to love the country. He was appalled to see good traditions, common dignity, functional practices, a workable economy, solemn religious practices, local and neighbourly ties—including long-standing property ties—torn asunder in a mass act of desecration, delinquency and discord.

Burke's most famous work, *Reflections on the Revolution in France*, was principally addressed to curtailing the influence of the French revolutionaries among the English, some of whom favoured applying the disruptive ideas to England. Additionally, Burke hoped to encourage and support his French friends and acquaintances who were either unsure about the revolution's merits or resistant to it.

He didn't offer a theoretical treatise on society and politics because speculative theories were the inadequate basis of the revolutionaries' tracts. Burke was a political empiricist: he wanted to see, to feel, to investigate for himself, to see what was already being done in each specific set of circumstances. It was necessary to have a sympathetic familiarity with matters before suggesting any gradual amendments to particular arrangements. More observing, more handling and testing, and further heuristic tinkering were required to judge the value, or faults, of those amendments. He knew this was a slow process, unlikely to impress the impatient; it lacked the spectacular advance and bold action of quick change. But Burke wanted to maintain all that had been attained and then to augment it rather than destroy it in the hope, always forlorn, of a totally new system.

Burke's understanding of the intricate, organic, creative, unplanned, surprising, local and personal nature of society informed his economic as well as his political thinking. Adam Smith, an acquaintance and admirer of Burke's, remarked that Burke seemed to have arrived independently at a similar economic understanding and grasped his—

Smith's—principles in a profound way. For example, Burke had the acuity to see how the money exchanged, prudently, between a lender and a hard-working borrower seeped and flowed in numerous small pathways that benefitted many more people than just the lender and borrower. It wasn't an exchange that forced servility on the lender; more often, it loosed restraints and allowed diligent work to prosper in wider, unexpected ways. Government intervention in these freely entered agreements between individuals would only sully and frustrate them. The best methods of regulation were informal: traditional customs, strongly embedded virtues and religious injunctions that promoted love for neighbour and denounced greed.

Burke was an anti-theorist although principles have been drawn legitimately from his thought. These principles include: trust those people adept at their work; distrust talkers who see only the negative aspects of anything; honour the achievements of the past that we've been blest to inherit; love the local and be wary of abstractions; good manners govern people better than fussy laws; each situation needing amendment is unique and therefore requires a specific response to bring improvement; government debt hampers effective action; if the majority of a nation's people are living in peace and enjoy a modicum of prosperity then no dramatic change is justified; any law that contradicts the temperament, customs, religion or reason of the broader population is a bad law. Burke was insistent that keeping foolish people from power was as important as raising good people to power. Militant atheists, in particular, were a powerful threat to order, justice and reasonable toleration; they were key players, hasty and reckless, in the French revolution.

This did not mean no change was helpful. Burke knew change was necessary to sustain and enhance existing goodness. For example, he admired the scientific and technological advances of his time. England was enjoying a tremendous period of invention and innovation: James Watt's steam engine designs freed industry from the low power and geographical limitations of water wheels; light iron ploughs, seeding machines, new crops from new lands and more efficient crop rotations brought huge increases in agricultural production to feed a burgeoning population; canals and improved roads facilitated transportation; the Royal Society was making exciting natural discoveries. New machines for improved textile manufacture stimulated new industries across England.

Burke welcomed the application of human intelligence to improve people's prosperity and freedoms. What he was against were attempts to usurp God's ordering of the world—expressed in nature and scripture, properly understood—and His purposeful design of humanity. Burke was opposed to any disregard for persistent human verities, including natural law and the peculiar human character. Always and everywhere people were reasonable but not exclusively so, closely linked to the past, primarily loyal to family and locality, creatures of habits and various guiding prejudices, limited in means, protectively self-interested, prone to pride and over-reach. Burke insisted that ignoring these crucial aspects of the human condition would always harm people.

Some writers with expertise on Burke, among them William Hazlitt and more recently Conor Cruise O'Brien, favoured reading much of Burke's voluminous writing to gain the fullest measure of his genius. No doubt this would produce readers with a broad and deep understanding of Edmund Burke's life and mind. The rejoinder is: who apart from a dedicated scholar has the time to labour—even if it's a valuable labour—in this way? The defence of this selection is that it gives an inviting taste of Burke's work. I hope many readers will afterwards proceed to read, at least, *Reflections on the Revolution in France*. If this selection does only that much it has justified its existence.

A benefit attached to reading Burke is acquaintance with the rich language of Georgian England. If we only read books of the last few decades we'll miss much of the Georgian age's precise, flexible and expressive mode of writing. Burke was a wise man, and he wrote with rare facility. His sentences are usually long, with many clauses, each one honing his point and providing nuance. Sometimes his prose demands careful attention to follow his point, but his writing always rewards the diligent. Like reading the novels of his younger compatriot Jane Austen, to read Burke is to immerse oneself in pages of discriminating eloquence grappling with universal human realities. This selection may take only an hour to two to read; it's likely to take many years of reflective experience to appreciate Burke's perspicacity.

It isn't a feature of this selection because the sober theme is political instruction, but Burke's humour is worth encountering. For example, when defending his right to defend himself against unjust accusations, Burke provides Job as an example: "The patience of Job is proverbial. After some of the convulsive struggles of our irritable nature, he submitted himself, and repented in dust and ashes. But even so, I do not find him blamed for reprehending, and with a considerable degree of verbal asperity, those ill-natured neighbours of his who visited his dunghill to read moral, political, and economical lectures on his misery." (*Letter to a Noble Lord*). Who among Australian politicians has this wit or this verbal asperity?

I hope my selection has abridged, but not emasculated Burke's writings, to quote the editor of an anthology from mid-last century. It would be possible to make a memorable book of Burke's arresting aphorisms, to deduct from his speeches, letters and books many sage and well-constructed single sentences. I have given, on the whole, longer selections because context is important. It was important to Burke's practical politics, and it honours his philosophy to maintain the context of his thoughts. Aiding this, the source of each selection is provided to place it in its broader context.

Throughout, the emphases are in the original works.

This selection is indebted to two previous selections: *Burke's Poetry & Prose* edited by A.M.D. Hughes, 1921; and, *Selections from the Speeches and Writings of Burke*, published by George Routledge & Co., 1853.

Gary Furnell

Notes on the source books/pamphlets for this selection

A Philosophical Enquiry into the Origin of Our Ideas of the Sublime and Beautiful, published in 1757. A treatise on aesthetics which garnered Burke some prominence as a writer and thinker.

The Present State of the Nation written in 1769 was Burke's assessment of the economic standing of England in response to the tax policies, which were aggravating rather than conciliatory, imposed on the American colonies.

Observations on a Late State of the Nation, 1769, was a response to George Grenville's pamphlet *The State of the Nation*. Burke argued for a free market embedded in traditional customs and manners; in contrast, government edicts were clumsy economic instruments.

Thoughts on the Cause of the Present Discontents, published 1770 to counter the actions of King George III who sought to dictate his will, via cronies, on the House of Commons.

Thoughts and Details on Scarcity was a memorandum about food shortages composed in 1775 to the Prime Minister, Mr. Pitt. Burke argued that the state should pursue a policy of minimum intervention in the marketplace, allowing the supply and demand to settle matters quickly, with private charities providing comfort and necessities to the sufferers.

Reflection on the Revolution in France, written in 1790, only one year after the revolution's outbreak. Burke sought to dampen enthusiasm for a similar revolution in England, and to warn of the dire consequences—among them, ruinous disorder leading to dictatorship—which he thought were the predictable outcome for the French.

An Appeal from the New to the Old Whigs, published in 1791. Burke wrote to defend his position against the French Revolution; some of his own party disagreed with his passionate condemnation of the drama unfolding in France.

Letters on a Regicide Peace, a 1795 series of letters to English political leaders, discouraging any attempt at accord with revolutionary France's rulers because France was hostile to Great Britain and intent on spreading revolution.

Excerpts from speeches and correspondence are noted.

1

PRACTICAL POLITICS

THE OBJECT OF THE STATE

The object of the state is (as far as may be) the happiness of the whole. Whatever makes multitudes of men utterly miserable can never answer that object; indeed it contradicts it wholly and entirely; and the happiness or misery of mankind, estimated by their feelings and sentiments, and not by any theories of their rights, is, and ought to be, the standard for the conduct of legislators towards the people. This naturally and necessarily conducts us to the peculiar and characteristic situation of a people, and to a knowledge of their opinions, prejudices, habits, and all the circumstances that diversify and colour life. The first question a good statesman would ask himself, therefore, would be, how and in what circumstances do you find the society, and to act upon them? (Speech to the House on Unitarians.)

NATURE AND FUNCTIONS OF THE HOUSE OF COMMONS.

The House of Commons was supposed originally to be *no part of the standing government of this country.* It was considered as a *control,* issuing *immediately* from the people, and speedily to be resolved into the mass from whence it arose. In this respect it was in the higher part of government what juries are in the lower. The capacity of a magistrate being transitory, and that of a citizen permanent, the latter capacity it was hoped would of course preponderate in all discussions, not only between the people and the standing authority of the crown, but between the people and the fleeting authority of the House of Commons itself. It was hoped that, being of a middle nature between subject and government, they would feel more tender and a nearer interest everything that concerned the people than the remoter and more permanent parts of legislature.

Whatever alterations time and the necessary accommodation of business may have introduced, this character can never be sustained, unless the House of Commons shall be made to bear some stamp of the actual disposition of the people at large. It would (among public misfortunes) be an evil more natural and tolerable, that the House of Commons should be infected with every epidemical frenzy of the people, as this would indicate some consanguinity, some sympathy of nature with their constituents, than that they should in all cases be wholly untouched by the opinions and feelings of the people out of doors. By this want of sympathy they would cease to be a house of commons. For it is not the derivation of the power of that house from the people, which makes it in a distinct sense their representative. The king is the representative of the people; so are the lords, so are the judges. They all are trustees for the people, as well as the commons; because no power is given for the sole sake of the holder; and although government certainly is an institution of Divine authority, yet its forms, and the persons who administer it, all originate from the people.

A popular origin cannot therefore be the characteristical distinction of a popular representative. This belongs equally to all parts of government, and in all forms. The virtue, spirit, and essence of a house of commons consists in its being the express image of the feelings of the nation. It was not instituted to be a control *upon* the people, as of late it has been taught, by a doctrine of the most pernicious tendency.

It was designed as a control *for* the people. Other institutions have been formed for the purpose of checking popular excesses; and they are, I apprehend, fully adequate to their object. If not, they ought to be made so. The House of Commons, as it was never intended for the support of peace and subordination, is miserably appointed for that service; having no stronger weapon than its mace, and no better officer than its serjeant-at-arms, which it can command of its own proper authority. A vigilant and jealous eye over executory[1] and judicial magistracy; an anxious care of public money; an openness, approaching towards facility, to public complaint; these seem to be the true characteristics of a house of commons. But an addressing house of commons, and a petitioning nation; a house of commons full of confidence, when the nation is plunged in despair; in the utmost harmony with ministers, whom the people regard with the utmost abhorrence; who vote thanks, when the public opinion calls upon them for impeachments; who are eager to grant, when the general voice demands account; who, in all disputes between the people and administration, presume against the people; who punish their disorders, but refuse even to inquire into the provocations to them; this is an unnatural, a monstrous state of things in this constitution.

Such an assembly may be a great, wise, awful senate; but it is not, to any popular purpose, a House of Commons. (*Thoughts on the Cause of the Present Discontents*).

---

1   Executory: public servants tasked with applying Parliament's decisions.

REVENUE *IS* THE STATE.

The revenue of the state is the state. In effect all depends upon it, whether for support or for reformation. The dignity of every occupation wholly depends upon the quantity and the kind of virtue that may be exerted on it. As all great qualities of the mind which operate in public, and are not merely suffering and passive, require force for their display, I had almost said for their unequivocal existence, the revenue, which is the spring of all power, becomes in its administration the sphere of every active virtue. Public virtue, being of a nature magnificent and splendid, instituted for great things, and conversant about great concerns, requires abundant scope and room, and cannot spread and grow under confinement, and in circumstances straitened, narrow, and sordid. Through the revenue alone the body politic can act in its true genius and character, and therefore it will display just as much of its collective virtue, and as much of its true genius and character, and therefore it will display just as much of that virtue which may characterize those who move it, and are, as it were, its life and guiding principle, as it is possessed of a just revenue. For from hence, not only magnanimity, and liberality, and beneficence, and fortitude, and providence, and the tutelary protection of all good arts, derive their food, and the growth of their organs, but continence, and self-denial, and labour, and vigilance, and frugality, and whatever else there is in which the mind shows itself above the appetite, are nowhere more in their proper element than in the provision and distribution of the public wealth. It is therefore not without reason that the science of speculative and practical finance, which must take to its aid so many auxiliary branches of knowledge, stands high in the estimation not only of the ordinary sort, but of the wisest and best men; and as this science has grown with the progress of its object, the prosperity and improvement of nations has generally increased with the increase of their revenues; and they will both continue to grow and flourish, as long as the balance between what is left to strengthen the efforts of individuals, and what is collected for the common efforts of the state, bear to each other a due reciprocal proportion, and are kept in close correspondence and communication...

The objects of the financier are, then, to secure and ample revenue; to impose it with judgement and equality; to employ it economically; and when necessity obliges him to make use of credit, to ensure its foundations in that instance, and for ever, by the clearness and candour of his proceedings, the exactness of his calculations, and the solidity of his funds. On these heads we may take a short and distinct view of the merits and abilities of those in the national assembly, who have taken to themselves the management of this arduous concern. (*Reflections on the Revolution in France*).

DEBT HAMPERS ACTION AND RECOVERY.

I am not in dread of the vast armies of France; I am not in dread of the gallant spirit of its brave and numerous nobility; I am not alarmed even at the great navy which has been so miraculously created. All these things Louis the Fourteenth had before. With all these things, the French monarchy has more than once fallen prostrate at the feet of the public faith of Great Britain. It was the want of public credit which disabled France from recovering after her defeats, or recovering even from her victories and triumphs. It was a prodigal court, it was an ill-ordered revenue, that sapped the foundations of all her greatness. Credit cannot exist under the arm of necessity. Necessity strikes at credit, I allow, with a heavier and quicker blow under an arbitrary monarchy, than under a limited and balanced government;

but still necessity and credit are natural enemies, and cannot be long reconciled in any situation. From necessity and corruption, a free state may lose the spirit of that complex constitution which is the foundation of confidence. (Speech to the House).

PATRIOTISM AND TAX.

Is it not the same virtue which does everything for us here in England? Do you imagine, then, that it is the land-tax which raises your revenue? that it is the annual vote in the committee of supply, which gives you your army? or that it is the Mutiny Bill, which inspires it with bravery and discipline? No! surely no! It is the love of the people; it is their attachment to their government, from the sense of the deep stake they have in such a glorious institution, which gives you your army and your navy, and infuses into both that liberal obedience, without which your army would be a base rabble, and your navy nothing but rotten timber.

All this, I know well enough, will sound wild and chimerical to the profane herd of those vulgar and mechanical politicians, who have no place among us; a sort of people who think that nothing exists but what is gross and material; and who therefore, far from being qualified to be directors of the great movement of empire, are not fit to turn a wheel in the machine. But to men truly initiated and rightly taught, these ruling and master principles, which, in the opinion of such men as I have mentioned, have no substantial existence, are in truth everything, and all in all. Magnanimity in politics is not seldom the truest wisdom; and a great empire and little minds go ill together. (Speech on Conciliation with the Colonies).

ECONOMIC REFORM.

As it is in the interest of the government that reformation should be early; it is the interest of the people that it should be temperate. It is their interest, because a temperate reform is permanent; and because it has a principle of growth. Whenever we improve, it is right to leave room for improvement. It is right to consider, to look about us, to examine the effect of what we have done. Then we can proceed with confidence, because we can proceed with intelligence. Whereas in hot reformations, in what men more zealous than considerate, call *making clear work*, the whole is generally so crude, so harsh, so indigested; mixed with so much imprudence, and so much injustice; so contrary to the whole course of human nature, and human institutions, that the very people who are most eager for it are among the first to grow disgusted at what they have done... A great part, therefore, of my idea of reform is meant to operate gradually; some benefits will come at a nearer, some at a more remote, period. We must no more make haste to be rich by parsimony, than by intemperate acquisition. (Speech to the House.)

A GOOD MEMBER OF PARLIAMENT.

To be a good member of parliament is, let me tell you, no easy task; especially at this time, when there is so strong a disposition to run into the perilous extremes of servile compliance or wild popularity. To unite circumspection with vigour is absolutely necessary; but it is extremely difficult. We are now members for a rich commercial *city*; this city, however, is but a part of a rich commercial *nation*, the interests of which are various, multiform, and intricate. We are members for that great nation, which however is itself but part of a great *empire*,

31

extended by our virtue and our fortune to the farthest limits of the east and of the west. All these wide-spread interests must be considered; must be compared; must be reconciled, if possible. We are members for a *free* country; and surely we all know, that the machine of a free constitution is no simple thing; but as intricate and as delicate as it is valuable. We are members in a great and ancient *monarchy*; and we must preserve religiously the true legal rights of the sovereign, which form the key-stone that binds together the noble and well-constructed arch of our empire and our constitution.

A representative worthy of you ought to be a person of stability. I am to look, indeed, to your opinions; but to such opinions as you and I must have five years hence. I was not to look to the flash of the day. I knew that you chose me, in my place, along with others, to be a pillar of the state, and not a weather-cock on the top of the edifice, exalted for my levity and versatility, and of no use but to indicate the shiftings of every fashionable gale. (Speech after the election of Bristol).

PRIVATE CHARACTER A BASIS FOR PUBLIC CONFIDENCE.

Before men are put forward into the great trusts of the state, they ought, by their conduct, to have obtained such a degree of estimation in their country, as may be some sort of pledge and security to the public, that they will not abuse those trusts. It is no mean security for a proper use of power, that a man has shown by the general tenor of his actions, that the affection, the good opinion, the confidence of his fellow citizens, have been among the principal objects of his life; and that he has owed none of the degradations of his power or fortune to a settled contempt, or occasional forfeiture of their esteem.

That man who before he comes into power has no friends, or who coming into power is obliged to desert his friends, or who losing it has no friends to sympathise with him; he who has no sway among any part of the landed or commercial interest, but whose whole importance has begun with his office, and is sure to end with it; is a person who ought never to be suffered by a controlling parliament to continue in any of those situations which confer the lead and direction of all our public affairs; because such a man *has no connexion with the interests of the people.*

Those knots or cabals of men who have got together avowedly without any public principle, in order to sell their conjunct iniquity at the higher rate, and are therefore universally odious, ought never to be suffered to domineer in the state; because they have *no connexion with the sentiments and opinions of the people. (Thoughts on the Cause of the Present Discontents).*

CHARACTER AND PUBLIC LIFE.

I remember an old scholastic aphorism which says, 'that the man who lives wholly detached from others must be either and angel or a devil.' When I see in any of these detached gentlemen of our times the angelic purity, power, and beneficence, I shall admit them to be angels. In the meantime we are born only to be men. We shall do good enough if we form ourselves to be good ones. It is therefore our business to carefully to cultivate in our minds, to rear to the most perfect vigour and maturity, every sort of generous and honest feeling that belongs to our nature. To bring the dispositions that are lovely in private life into the service and conduct of the commonwealth; so to be patriots, as not to forget that we are gentlemen. To cultivate friendships, and to incur enmities. To have both strong, but both selected; in the one to be placable; in the other immovable. To model our principles to our duties and our situation. To be fully persuaded that all virtue that is impracticable is spurious; and rather to run the risk of falling into faults in the course which leads us to act with effect and energy, than to loiter out our days without blame and without use. Public life is a situation of power and energy; he trespasses against his duty who sleeps on his watch, as well as he that goes over to the enemy. (*Thoughts on the Cause of the Present Discontents*).

VIRTUE AND WISDOM QUALIFY FOR GOVERNMENT.

There is no qualification for government but virtue and wisdom, actual or presumptive. Wherever they are actually found, they have, in whatever state, condition, profession, or trade, the passport of heaven to human place and honour. Woe to that country which would madly and impiously reject the service of the talents and virtues, civil, military, or religious, that are given to grace and to serve it; and would condemn to obscurity everything formed to diffuse lustre and glory around a state. Woe to that country, too, that, passing into the opposite extreme, considers a low education, a mean, contracted view of things, a sordid, mercenary occupation, as a preferable title to command. Everything ought to be open; but not indifferently to every man. No rotation; no appointment by lot; no mode of election operating in the spirit of sortition, or rotation, can be generally good in a government conversant in extensive objects. Because they have no tendency, direct or indirect, to select the man with a view to the duty, or to accommodate the one to the other. I do not hesitate to say, that the road to eminence and power, from obscure condition, ought not to be made too easy, nor a thing too much of course. If rare merit be the rarest of all rare things, in ought to pass through some sort of probation. The temple of honour ought to be seated on an eminence. If it be opened through virtue, let it be remembered, too, that virtue is never tried but by some difficulty and some struggle. (*Reflections on the Revolution in France*).

INTRIGUERS DISQUALIFIED FOR GOVERNMENT.

I have known merchants with the sentiments and the abilities of great statesmen; and I have seen persons in the rank of statesmen, with the conceptions and character of pedlars. Indeed, my observation has furnished me with nothing that is to be found in any habits of life or education, which tends wholly to disqualify men for the functions of government, but that, by which the power of exercising those functions is very frequently obtained. I mean, a spirit and habits of low cabal and intrigue; which I have never, in one instance, seen united with a capacity for sound and manly policy. (Speech to the House on India).

EXCLUDE FOOLISH PEOPLE.

Every good political institution must have a preventive operation as well as a remedial. It ought to have a natural tendency to exclude bad men from government, and not to trust for the safety of the state to subsequent punishment alone: punishment, which has ever been tardy and uncertain, and which, when power is suffered in bad hands, may chance to fall rather on the injured than the criminal. (*Thoughts on the Cause of the Present Discontents*).

PREPARATION FOR PARLIAMENT.

When I first devoted myself to the public service, I considered how I should render myself fit for it; and this I did by endeavouring to discover what it was that gave this country the rank it holds in the world. I found that our prosperity and dignity arose principally, if not solely, from two sources;—our constitution and commerce. Both these I have spared no study to understand, and no endeavour to support.

The distinguishing part of our constitution is its liberty. To preserve that liberty inviolate, seems the particular duty and proper trust of a member of the House of Commons. But the liberty, the only liberty I mean, is a liberty connected with order; that not only exists along with order and virtue, but which cannot exist at all without them. It inheres in good and steady government, as in its substance and vital principle.

The other source of our power is commerce, of which you are so large a part, and which cannot exist, no more than your liberty, without a connection with many virtues. It has ever been a very particular and a very favourite object of my study, in its principles, and in its details. I think many here are acquainted with the truth of what I say.

This I know, that I have ever had my house open, and my poor services ready, for traders and manufacturers of every denomination. My favourite ambition is to have those services acknowledged. I now appear before you to make trial, whether my earnest endeavours have been so wholly oppressed by the weakness of my abilities as to be rendered insignificant in the eyes of a great trading city; or whether you choose to give a weight to humble abilities, for the sake of the honest exertions with which they are accompanied. This is my trial to-day.

My industry is not on trial. Of my industry I am sure, as far as my constitution of mind and body admitted. (Speech to the electors of Bristol).

ONE PARLIAMENT.

Parliament is not a *congress* of ambassadors from different and hostile interests, which interests each must maintain, as an agent and advocate, against other agents and advocates; but parliament is a *deliberative* assembly of *one* nation, with *one* interest, that of the whole; where, not local purposes, not local prejudices, ought to guide, but the general good, resulting from the general reason of the whole. You choose a member indeed; but when you have chosen him, he is not member of Bristol, but he is a member of *Parliament*. If the local constituent should have an interest, or should form an hasty opinion, evidently opposite to the real good of the rest of the community, the member for that place ought to be as far, as any other, from any endeavour to give it effect. I beg pardon for saving so much on this subject. I have been unwillingly drawn into it; but I shall ever use a respectful frankness of communication with you. Your faithful friend, your devoted servant, I shall be to the end of my life: a flatterer you do not wish for. On this point of instructions, however, I think it scarcely possible, we ever can have any sort of difference. Perhaps I may give you too much, rather than too little trouble. (Speech to the electors of Bristol).

PEOPLE AND PARLIAMENT.

Let the commons in parliament assembled be one and the same thing with the commons at large. The distinctions that are made to separate us are unnatural and wicked contrivances. Let us identify, let us incorporate, ourselves with the people. Let us cut all the cables and snap the chains which tie us to an unfaithful shore, and enter the friendly harbour that shoots far out into the main its moles and jettees to receive us. "War with the world, and peace with our constituents."

Be this our motto, and our principle. Then, indeed, we shall be truly great. Respecting ourselves, we shall be respected by the world. At present all is troubled, and cloudy, and distracted, and full of anger and turbulence, both abroad and at home; but the air may be cleared by this storm, and light and fertility may follow it. Let us give a faithful pledge to the people, that we honour indeed the crown, but that we *belong* to them; that we are their auxiliaries, and not their task-masters,—the fellow-labourers in the same vineyard,—not lording over their rights, but helpers of their joy: that to tax them is a grievance to ourselves; but to cut off from our enjoyments to forward theirs, is the highest gratification we are capable of receiving. (Speech after the election at Bristol).

VOICE OF THE PEOPLE.

Government is deeply interested in everything which, even through the medium of some temporary uneasiness, may tend finally to compose the minds of the subjects, and to conciliate their affections. I have nothing to do here with the abstract value of the voice of the people.

But as long as reputation, the most precious possession of every individual, and as long as opinion, the great support of the state, depend entirely upon that voice, it can never be considered as a thing of little consequence either to individuals or to governments. Nations are not primarily ruled by laws; less by violence. Whatever original energy may be supposed either in force or regulation, the operation of both is, in truth, merely instrumental. Nations are governed by the same methods, and on the same principles, by which an individual without authority is often able to govern those who are his equals or his superiors—by a knowledge of their temper, and by a judicious management of it; I mean, when public affairs are steadily and quietly conducted; and when government is nothing but a continued scuffle between the magistrate and the multitude; in which sometimes the one and sometimes the other is uppermost; in which they alternately yield and prevail, in a series of contemptible victories, and scandalous submissions. The temper of the people amongst whom he presides ought therefore to be the first study of a statesman. And the knowledge of this temper it is by no means impossible for him to attain, if he has not an interest in being ignorant of what it is his duty to learn.

To complain of the age we live in, to murmur at the present possessors of power, to lament the past, to conceive extravagant hopes of the future, are the common dispositions of the greater part of mankind— indeed, the necessary effects of the ignorance and levity of the vulgar. Such complaints and humours have existed in all times; yet as all times have *not* been alike, true political sagacity manifests itself, in distinguishing that complaint which only characterises the general infirmity of human nature from those which are symptoms of the particular distemperature of our own air and season. (*Thoughts on the Cause of the Present Discontents*).

THE PEOPLE AND THEIR RULERS.

I am not one of those who think that the people are never in the wrong. They have been so, frequently and outrageously, both in other countries and in this. But I do say, that in all disputes between them and their rulers, the presumption is at least upon a par in favour of the people. Experience may perhaps justify me in going farther. When popular discontents have been very prevalent, it may well be affirmed and supported, that there has been generally something found amiss in the constitution, or in the conduct of government. The people have no interest in disorder. When they do wrong, it is their error, and not their crime. But with the governing part of the state it is far otherwise. They certainly may act ill by design, as well as by mistake. (*Thoughts on the Cause of the Present Discontents*).

POWER OF CONSTITUENTS.

The power of the people, within the laws, must show itself sufficient to protect every representative in the animated performance of his duty, or that duty cannot be performed. The House of Commons can never be a control on other parts of government, unless they are controlled themselves by their constituents; and unless these constituents possess some right in the choice of that house, which it is not in the power of that house to take away. If they suffer this power of arbitrary incapacitation to stand, they have utterly perverted every other power of the House of Commons. The late proceeding I will not say *is* contrary to law, it *must* be so; for the power which is claimed cannot, by any possibility, be a legal power in any limited member of government. (*Thoughts on the Cause of the Present Discontents*).

CONFIDENCE *IN* THE PEOPLE, CONFIDENCE *OF* THE PEOPLE.

They may be assured, that however they amuse themselves with a variety of projects for substituting something else in the place of that great and only foundation of government, the confidence of the people, every attempt will but make their condition worse. When men imagine that their food is only a cover for poison, and when they neither love nor trust the hand that serves it, it is not the name of the roast beef of Old England, that will persuade them to sit down to the table that is spread for them.

When the people conceive that laws, and tribunals, and even popular assemblies, are perverted from the ends of their institution, they find in those names of degenerated establishments only new motives to discontent. Those bodies which, when full of life and beauty, lay in their arms, and were their joy and comfort, when dead and putrid, become but the more loathsome from remembrance of former endearments. A sullen gloom and furious disorder prevail by fits: the nation loses its relish for peace and prosperity; as it did in that season of fullness which opened our troubles in the time of Charles the First. A species of men to whom a state of order would become a sentence of obscurity, are nourished into a dangerous magnitude by the heat of intestine disturbances; and it is no wonder that, by a sort of sinister piety, they cherish, in their turn, the disorders which are the parents of all their consequence. (*Thoughts on the Cause of the Present Discontents*).

THE PRESUMPTION OF SETTLED GOVERNMENT.

It is a presumption in favour of any settled scheme of government against any untried project that a nation has long existed and flourished under it. It is a better presumption even of the choice of a nation, far better than any sudden and temporary arrangement by actual election. Because a nation is not an idea only of local extent and individual momentary aggregation, but it is an idea of continuity which extends in time as well as in numbers and in space. And this is not a choice of one day, or one set of people, not a tumultary and giddy choice; it is a constitution made by what is ten thousand times better than choice, it is made by the peculiar circumstances, occasions, tempers, dispositions, and moral, civil, and social habititudes of the people, which disclose themselves only in a long space of time. It is a vestment which accommodates itself to the body. Nor is prescription of government formed upon blind unmeaning prejudices—for man is a most unwise and wise being. The individual is foolish. The multitude, for the moment, is so foolish when they act without deliberation; but the species is wise, and when time is given to it, as a species, it almost always acts right... (*The Present State of the Nation*).

THE PROVINCE OF GOVERNMENT.

It is one of the finest problems in legislation, and what has often engaged my thoughts whilst I followed that profession, 'what the state ought to take upon itself to direct by the public wisdom, and what it ought to leave, with as little interference as possible, to individual discretion'. Nothing, certainly, can be laid down on the subject that will not admit of exceptions, many permanent, some occasional. But the clearest line of distinction which I could draw whilst I had my chalk to draw any line, was this; that the state ought to confine itself to what regards the state, namely, the exterior establishments of its religion; its magistracy; its revenue; it military force by sea and land; the corporations that owe their existence to its fiat; in a word, to everything that is *truly and properly* public, to the public peace, to the public safety, to the public prosperity. In its preventive police it ought to be sparing in its efforts and employ means, rather few, unfrequent and strong, than many and frequent, and of course, as they multiply their puny politic race and dwindle, small and feeble. Statesmen who know themselves will, with the dignity that belongs to wisdom, proceed only in this the superior orb, and first mover of their duty steadily, vigilantly, severely, courageously: whatever remains will, in a manner, provide for itself. But as they descend from the state to the province, from a province to a parish, and from a parish to a private house, they go on accelerated in their fall. They *cannot* do the lower duty; and, in proportion as they try it, they will certainly fail in the higher. They ought to know the different departments of things; what belongs to laws, and what manners alone can regulate. To these great politicians may give a leaning, but they cannot give a law. (*Thoughts and Details on Scarcity*).

CORRECTING PARLIAMENTARY DISORDERS

The distempers of the monarchy were the great subjects of apprehension and redress in the last century; in this, the distempers of parliament. It is not in parliament alone that the remedy for parliamentary disorders can be completed; hardly indeed can it begin there. Until a confidence in government is re-established, the people ought to be excited to a more strict and detailed attention to the conduct of their representatives. Standards for judging more systematically upon their conduct ought to be settled in the meetings of counties and corporations. Frequent and correct lists of the voters in all important questions ought to be procured.

By such means something may be done. By such means it may appear who those are that, by an indiscriminate support of all administrators, have totally banished all integrity and confidence out of public proceedings; have confounded the best men with the worst; and weakened and dissolved, instead of strengthening and compacting, the general frame of government. (*Thoughts on the Cause of the Present Discontents*).

PUBLIC SALARY FOR POLITICIANS AND PUBLIC SERVANTS.

I am not possessed of an exact common measure between real service and its reward. I am very sure that states do sometimes receive services which it is hardly in their power to reward according to their worth. If I were to give my judgment with regard to this country, I do not think the great efficient offices of the state to be overpaid. The service of the public is a thing which cannot be put to auction, and struck down to those who will agree to execute it the cheapest. When the proportion between reward and service is our object, we must always consider of what nature the service is, and what sort of men they are that must perform it. What is just payment for one kind of labour, and full encouragement for one kind of talents, is fraud and discouragement to others. Many of the great offices have much duty to do, and much expense of representation to maintain. A secretary of state, for instance, must not appear sordid in the eyes of the ministers of other nations; neither ought our ministers abroad to appear contemptible in the courts where they reside. In all offices of duty, there is, almost necessarily, a great neglect of all domestic affairs. A person in high office can rarely take a view of his family house. If he sees that the state takes no detriment, the state must see that his affairs should take as little.

I will even go so far as to affirm, that if men were willing to serve in such situations without salary, they ought not to be permitted to do it. Ordinary service must be secured by the motives to ordinary integrity. I do not hesitate to say, that that state which lays its foundations in rare and heroic virtues, will be sure to have its superstructure in the basest profligacy and corruption. An honourable and fair profit is the best security against avarice and rapacity; as in all things else, a lawful and regulated enjoyment is the best security against debauchery and excess. For as wealth is power, so all power will infallibly draw wealth to itself by some means or other: and when men are left no way of ascertaining their profits but by their means of obtaining them, those means will be increased to infinity. This is true in all the parts of administration, as well as in the whole. If any individual were to decline his appointments, it might give an unfair advantage to ostentatious ambition over unpretending service; it might breed invidious comparisons; it might tend to destroy whatever little unity and agreement may be found among ministers. And, after all, when an ambitious man had run down his competitors by a fallacious show of disinterestedness, and fixed himself in power by that means, what security is there that he would not change his course, and claim as an indemnity ten times more than he has given up? (Speech to the House on economic reform).

TRUE AND FALSE COALITIONS.

No system of that kind can be formed, which will not leave room fully sufficient for an healing coalition: but no coalition which, under the specious name of independency, carries in its bosom the unreconciled principles of the original discord of parties, ever was, or will be, an healing coalition. Nor will the mind of our sovereign ever know repose, his kingdom settlement, or his business order, in efficiency or grace with his people, until things are established upon the basis of some set of men, who are trusted by the public, and who can trust one another. (*Observations on a Late State of the Nation*).

PARTY AND LOYALTY.

Party is a body of men united, for promoting by their joint endeavours the national interest, upon some particular principle in which they are all agreed. For my part, I find it impossible to conceive that any one believes in his own politics, or thinks them to be of any weight, who refuses to adopt the means of having them reduced into practice. It is the business of the speculative philosopher to mark the proper ends of government. It is the business of the politician, who is the philosopher in action, to find out proper means towards those ends, and to employ them with effect. Therefore every honourable connection will avow it is their first purpose to pursue every just method to put the men who hold their opinions into such a condition as may enable them to carry their common plans into execution, with all the power and authority of the state. As this power is attached to certain situations, it is their duty to contend for these situations. Without a proscription of others, they are bound to give to their own party the preference in all things; and by no means, for private considerations, to accept any offers of power in which the whole body is not included; nor to suffer themselves to be led, or to be controlled, or to be overbalanced, in office or in council, by those who contradict the very fundamental principles on which their party is formed, and even those upon which every fair connection must stand. Such a generous contention for power, on such manly and honourable maxims, will easily be distinguished from the mean and interested struggle for place and emolument. The very style of such persons will serve to discriminate them from those numberless imposters who have deluded the ignorant with professions incompatible with human practice, and have afterwards incensed them by practices below the level of vulgar rectitude. (*Thoughts on the Cause of the Present Discontents*).

A PARTY MAN.

The only method which has ever been found effectual to preserve any man against the corruption of nature and example, is a habit of life and communication of counsels with the most virtuous and public-spirited men of the age you live in. Such a society cannot be kept without advantage or deserted without shame. For this rule of conduct I may be called in reproach a *party man*; but I am little affected with such aspersions. In the way which they call party, I worship the constitution of your fathers; and I shall never blush for my political company. All reverence to honour, all idea of what it is, will be lost out of the world, before it can be imputed as a fault to any man, that he has been closely connected with those incomparable persons, living and dead, with whom for eleven years I have constantly thought and acted. (Letter to Sheriffs[2] of Bristol on affairs in America).

POLITICAL CONNECTIONS AND GOOD POLICIES.

Every profession, not excepting the glorious one of a soldier, or the sacred one of a priest, is liable to its own particular vices, which, however, form no argument against those ways of life; nor are the vices themselves inevitable to every individual in those professions. Of such a nature are connections in politics; essentially necessary for the full performance of our public duty, accidentally liable to degenerate into faction. Commonwealths are made of families, free commonwealths of parties also; and we may as well affirm, that our natural regards and ties of blood tend inevitably to make men bad citizens, as that the bonds of our party weaken those by which we are held to our country.

---

2   Sheriffs were local officials with important administrative and legal roles. They operated on the King's behalf.

Some legislators went so far as to make neutrality in party a crime against the state. I do not know whether this might not have been rather to overstrain the principle. Certain it is, the best patriots in the greatest commonwealths have always commended and promoted such connections. *Idem sentire de republica*[3], was with them a principal ground of friendship and attachment; nor do I know any other capable of forming firmer, dearer, more pleasing, more honourable, and more virtuous habitudes. The Romans carried this principle a great way. Even the holding of offices together, the disposition of which arose from chance, not selection, gave rise to a relation which continued for life. It was called *necessitudo sortis*[4]; and it was looked upon with a sacred reverence. Breaches of any of these kinds of civil relation were considered as acts of the most distinguished turpitude. The whole people was distributed into political societies, in which they acted in support of such interests in the state as they severally affected. For it was then thought no crime to endeavour, by every honest means, to advance to superiority and power those of your own sentiments and opinions. This wise people was far from imagining that those connections had no tie, and obliged to no duty; but that men might quit them without shame, upon every call of interest. They believed private honour to be the great foundation of public trust; that friendship was no mean step towards patriotism; that he who, in the common intercourse of life, showed he regarded somebody besides himself, when he came to act in a public situation, might probably consult some other interest than his own. (*Thoughts on the Present Discontents*).

---

3   Cicero: Latin for *Everyone will share the same opinion about public affairs.*

4   Latin: *The necessity of fate.*

AN ENTRANCING NEUTRALITY.

They were a race of men (I hope in God the species is extinct) who, when they rose in their place, no man living could divine, from any known adherence to parties, to opinions, or to principles, from any order or system in their politics, or from any sequel or connection in their ideas, what part they were going to take in any debate. It is astonishing how much this uncertainty, especially at critical times, called the attention of all parties on such men. All eyes were fixed on them, all ears open to hear them; each party gaped, and looked alternately for their vote, almost to the end of their speeches. While the house hung on this uncertainty, now the *hear hims* rose from this side—now they rebellowed from the other; and that party, to whom they fell at length from their tremulous and dancing balance, always received them in a tempest of applause. The fortune of such men was a temptation too great to be resisted by one to whom a single whiff of incense withheld gave much greater pain than he received delight in the clouds of it which daily rose about him from the prodigal superstition of innumerable admirers. He was a candidate for contradictory honours; and his great aim was to make those agree in admiration of him who never agreed in anything else. (Speech to the House on American taxation).

INSTABILITY FROM FREQUENT CHANGE.

Let us learn from our experience. It is not support that is wanting to government, but reformation. When ministry rests upon public opinion, it is not indeed built upon a rock of adamant; it has, however, some stability. But when it stands upon private humour, its structure is of stubble, and its foundation is on quicksand. I repeat it again—He that supports every administration subverts all government. The reason is this: The whole business in which a court usually takes an interest goes on at present equally well, in whatever hands, whether high or low, wise or foolish, scandalous or reputable; there is nothing, therefore, to hold it firm to any one body of men, or to any one consistent scheme of politics. Nothing interposes to prevent the full operation of all the caprices and all the passions of a court upon the servants of the public. The system of administration is open to continual shocks and changes, upon the principles of the meanest cabal, and the most contemptible intrigue. Nothing can be solid and permanent. All good men at length fly with horror from such a service. Men of rank and ability, with the spirit which ought to animate such men in a free state, while they decline the jurisdiction of dark cabal on their actions and their fortunes, will, for both, cheerfully put themselves upon their country.

They will trust an inquisitive and distinguishing parliament; because it does inquire, and does distinguish. If they act well, they know that, in such a parliament, they will be supported against any intrigue; if they act ill, they know that no intrigue can protect them. This situation, however awful, is honourable. But in one hour, and in the self-same assembly, without any assigned or assignable cause, to be precipitated from the highest authority to the most marked neglect, possibly into the greatest peril of life and reputation, is a situation full of danger, and destitute of honour. It will be shunned equally by every man of prudence, and every man of spirit.

By this unprincipled facility of changing the state as often, and as much, and in as many ways as there are floating fancies or passions, the whole chain and continuity of the commonwealth would be broken. No one generation could link with the other. Man would become little better than flies of the summer... Nothing stable in the modes of holding property, or exercising function, could form a solid ground on which any parent could speculate in the education of his offspring, or in choice for their future establishment in the world. No principles could be early worked into the habits. As soon as the most able instructor had completed his laborious course on institution, instead of sending forth his pupil, accomplished in a virtuous discipline, fitted to procure him attention and respect, in his place in society, he would find every thing altered; and that he had turned out a poor creature to the contempt and derision of the world, ignorant of the true grounds of estimation. Who would insure a tender and delicate sense of honour to beat almost with the first pulses of the heart, when no man could know what would be the test of honour in a nation, continually varying the standard of its coin? No part of life would retain its acquisitions. Barbarism with regard to science and literature, unskillfulness with regard to arts and manufactures, would infallibly succeed to the want of a steady education and settled principle; and thus the commonwealth itself would, in a few generations, crumble away, be disconnected into the dust and powder of individuality, and at length be dispersed to all the winds of heaven.

To avoid therefore the evils of inconstancy and versatility, ten thousand times worse than those of obstinacy and the blindest prejudice, we have consecrated the state, that no man should approach to look at its defects or corruption but with due caution; that he should never dream of beginning its reformation by its subversion; that he should approach to the faults of the state as to the wounds of a father, with pious awe and trembling solicitude. Those who are prompt act rashly to hack that aged parent in pieces, and put him into the kettle of magicians, in hopes that by poisonous weeds and wild incantation, they may regenerate the paternal constitution, and renovate their father's life.

Society is indeed a contract. Subordinate contracts for objects of mere occasional interest may be dissolved at pleasure—but the state ought not to be considered as nothing better than a partnership agreement in a trade of pepper and coffee, calico or tobacco, or some other such low concern, to be taken up for a little temporary interest, and to be dissolved by the fancy of the parties. It is to be looked on with reverence; because it is not a partnership in things subservient only to the gross animal existence of a temporary and perishable nature. It is a partnership of all science; a partnership of all art; a partnership of every virtue, and in all perfection. As the ends of such a partnership cannot be obtained in many generations, it becomes a partnership not only between those who are living, but between those who are living, those who are dead, and those who are to be born. (*Reflections on the Revolution in France*).

PATIENCE ACHIEVES MORE THAN FORCE.

But you might object—'A process of this kind is slow. It is not fit for an assembly, which glories in performing in a few months the work of ages. Such a mode of reforming, possibly might take up many years.' Without question it might; and it ought. It is one of the excellencies of a method in which time is amongst the assistants, that its operation is slow, and in some cases almost imperceptible. If circumspection and caution are a part of wisdom, when we work only upon inanimate matter, surely they become part of duty too, when the subject of our demolition and construction is not brick and timber, but sentient beings, by the sudden alteration of whose state, condition, and habits, multitudes might be rendered miserable ... The true lawgiver ought to have a heart full of sensibility. He ought to love and respect his kind, and to fear himself. It may be allowed to his temperament to catch his ultimate object with an intuitive glance; but his movements towards it ought to be deliberate. Political arrangement, as it is a work for social ends, is to be only wrought by social means. There, mind must conspire with mind. Time is required to produce that union of minds which time alone can produce all the good that we aim at. Our patience will achieve more than our force ... I have never yet seen any plan which has not yet been mended by the observations of those who were much inferior in understanding to the person who took the lead in the business. By a slow but well-sustained progress, the effect of each step is watched; the good or ill success of the first gives light to us in the second; and so, from light to light, we are conducted with safety through the whole series. We see the parts or the system through the whole series. We see that the parts or the system do not clash. The evils latent in the most promising contrivances are provided for as they arise. One advantage is as little as possible is sacrificed for another. We compensate, we reconcile, we balance. We are enabled to unite into a consistent whole the various anomalies and contending principles that are found in the minds and affairs of men. From hence arises, not an excellence in simplicity, but one far superior, an excellence in composition. (*Reflections on the Revolution in France*).

THE MIDDLE WAY.

There is something else than the mere alternative of absolute destruction or unreformed existence. *Spartam nactum es, hanc exorna.*[5] This is, in my opinion, a rule of profound sense, and ought never to depart the mind of an honest reformer. I cannot conceive how any man can have brought himself to that pitch of presumption, to consider his country nothing but *carte blanche*, upon which he

---

5   Euripides, from the play, *Telephus:* You have obtained Sparta: adorn it.

may scribble whatever he pleases. A man full of warm speculative benevolence may wish his society otherwise constituted than he finds it; but a good patriot, and a true politician, always considers how he shall make the most of the existing materials of his country. A disposition to preserve, and an ability to improve, taken together, would be my standard of a statesman. Every thing else is vulgar in the conception, perilous in the execution. (*Reflections on the Revolution in France*).

SAFETY IN COMBINATION, NOT FACTION.

That connection and faction are equivalent terms, is an opinion which has been carefully inculcated at all times by unconstitutional statesmen. The reason is evident. Whilst men are linked together, they easily and speedily communicate the alarm of any evil design. They are enabled to fathom it with common counsel, and to oppose it with united strength. Whereas, when they lie dispersed, without concert, order, or discipline, communication is uncertain, counsel difficult, and resistance impracticable. Where men are not acquainted with each other's principles, nor experienced in each other's talents, nor at all practised in their mutual habitudes and dispositions by joint efforts in business; no personal confidence, no friendship, no common interest, subsisting among them; it is evidently impossible that they can act a public part with uniformity, perseverance, or efficacy. In a connection, the most inconsiderable man, by adding to the weight of the whole, has his value, and his use; out of it, the greatest talents are wholly unserviceable to the public. No man, who is not inflamed by vain-glory into enthusiasm, can flatter himself that his single, unsupported, desultory, unsystematic endeavours, are of power to defeat the subtle designs and united cabals of ambitious citizens. When bad men combine, the good must associate; else they will fall, one by one, an unpitied sacrifice in a contemptible struggle. (*Thoughts on the Cause of the Present Discontents*).

SOBRIETY IN PARTY DIVISIONS.

Party divisions, whether on the whole operating for good or evil, are things inseparable from free government. This is a truth which, I believe, admits little dispute, having been established by the uniform experience of all ages. The part a good citizen ought to take in these divisions has been a matter of much deeper controversy. But God forbid that any controversy relating to our essential morals should admit of no decision. It appears to me, that this question, like most of the others which regard our duties in life, is to be determined by our station in it. Private men may be wholly neutral, and entirely innocent; but they who are legally invested with public trust, or stand on the high ground of rank and dignity, which is trust implied, can hardly in any case remain indifferent, without the certainty of sinking into insignificance; and thereby in effect deserting that post in which, with the fullest authority, and for the wisest purposes, the laws and institutions of their country have fixed them. However, if it be the office of those who are thus circumstanced, to take a decided part, it is no less their duty that it should be a sober one. (*Observations on a Late State of the Nation*).

POLITICAL EMPIRICISM.

Men of sense, when new projects come before them, always think a discourse proving the mere right or mere power of acting in the manner proposed, to be no more than a very unpleasant way of misspending time.

They must see the object to be of proper magnitude to engage them; they must see the means of compassing it to be next to certain: the mischiefs not to counterbalance the profit; they will examine how a proposed imposition or regulation agrees with the opinion of those who are likely to be affected by it; they will not despise the consideration even of their habitudes and prejudices. They wish to know how it accords or disagrees with the true spirit of prior establishments, whether of government or of finance; because they well know, that in the complicated economy of great kingdoms, and immense revenues, which in a length of time, and by a variety of accidents, have coalesced into a sort of body, an attempt towards a compulsory equality in all circumstances, and an exact practical definition of the supreme rights in every case, is the most dangerous and chimerical of all enterprises. The old building stands well enough, though part Gothic, part Grecian, and part Chinese, until an attempt is made to square it into uniformity. Then it may come down upon our heads altogether, in much uniformity of ruin; and great will be the fall thereof. (*Thoughts on the Cause of the Present Discontents*).

GOVERNMENT FAVOURITISM.

A plan of favouritism for our executory government is essentially at variance with the plan of our legislature. One great end undoubtedly of a mixed government like ours, composed of monarchy, and of controls, on the part of the higher people and the lower, is that the prince shall not be able to violate the laws. This is useful indeed and fundamental.

But this, even at first view, in no more than a negative advantage; an armour merely defensive. It is therefore next in order, and equal in importance, that the discretionary powers which are necessarily vested in the monarch, whether for the execution of the laws, or for the nomination to magistracy and office, or for the conducting of the affairs of peace and war, or for ordering the revenue, should all be exercised upon public principles and national grounds, and not on the likings or prejudices, the intrigues or policies, of a court[6]. (*Thoughts on the Cause of the Present Discontents*).

PUBLIC SERVANTS CORRESPONDENT TO GOVERNMENT.

In arbitrary governments, the constitution of the ministry follows the constitution of the legislature. Both the law and the magistrate are the creatures of will. It must be so. Nothing, indeed, will appear more certain, on any tolerable consideration of this matter, than that every sort of government ought to have its administration correspondent to its legislature.

If it should be otherwise, things must fall into a hideous disorder. The people of a free commonwealth, who have taken such care that their laws should be the result of general consent, cannot be so senseless as to suffer their executory system to be composed of persons on whom they have no dependence, and whom no proofs of the public love and confidence have recommended to those powers, upon the use of which the very being of the state depends. (*Thoughts*

---

6   Court: courtiers, or clique of powerful people.

on the Cause of the Present Discontents).

Nothing can render this a point of indifference to the nation, but what must either render us totally desperate, or sooth us into the security of idiots. We must soften into a credulity below the milkiness of infancy, to think all men virtuous. We must be tainted with a malignity truly diabolical, to believe all the world to be equally wicked and corrupt. Men are in public as in private, some good, some evil. The elevation of the one, and the depression of the other, are the first objects of all true policy. But that form of government, which, neither in its direct institutions, nor in their immediate tendency, has contrived to throw its affairs into the most trustworthy hands, but has left its whole executory system to be disposed of agreeably to the uncontrolled pleasures of any one man, however excellent or virtuous, is a plan of polity defective not only in that member, but consequentially erroneous in every part of it. (*Thoughts on the Cause of the Present Discontents*).

NEW POWERS ALLIED WITH THE PRESS

[In France] a silent revolution in the moral world preceded the political, and prepared it. It became of more importance than ever what examples were given, and what measures were adopted. Their causes no longer lurked in the recesses of cabinets, or in the private conspiracies of the factious. They were no longer controlled by the force and influence of the grandees, who had formerly been able to stir up troubles by their discontents, and to quiet them by their corruption. The chain of subordination, even in cabal and sedition, was broken in its most important links. It was no longer the great and the populace. Other interests were formed, other dependencies, other connexions, other communications. The middle classes had swelled far beyond their former proportion. Like whatever is the most effectively rich and great in society, these classes became the seat of all the active politics, and the preponderating weight to decide on them. There were all the energies by which fortune is acquired; there are the consequence of their success. There were all the talents which assert their pretensions, and are impatient of the place which settled society prescribed to them. These descriptions got between the great and the populace; and the influence on the lower classes was with them. The spirit of ambition had taken possession of this class as violently as ever it had done of any other. They felt the importance of this situation. The correspondence of the monied and mercantile world, the literary intercourse of academics, but above all, the press, of which they [the middle class rebels] had in a manner entire possession, made a kind of electric communication everywhere. The press in reality has made every government, in its spirit, democratic[7]. Without it the great, the first movements in this Revolution could not, perhaps, have been given. But the spirit of ambition, now for the first time connected with the spirit of speculation, was not to be restrained at will. There was no longer any means of arresting a principle in its course. (*Letters on a Regicide Peace*).

THE CHIRPING GRASSHOPPERS.

The vanity, restlessness, petulance, and spirit of intrigue, of several petty cabals, who attempt to hide their total want of consequence in bustle and noise and puffing and mutual quotation of each other, makes you imagine that our contemptuous neglect of their abilities is a general mark of our acquiescence in their opinions. No such thing, I assure you. Because half a dozen grasshoppers under a fern make

---

7   For Burke, this wasn't necessarily good; a democratic spirit may be a manipulated or reckless spirit.

the field ring with their importunate chink, whilst thousands of great cattle, reposed beneath the shadow of the British oak, chew their cud and are silent, pray do not imagine that those who make the noise are the only inhabitants of the field; that of course they are many in number; or that, after all, they are other than the little, shrivelled, meagre, hopping, though loud and troublesome insects of the hour. (*Reflections on the Revolution in France*).

INFLUENCES IN GOVERNMENT.

It is no inconsiderable part of wisdom, to know how much of an evil ought to be tolerated; lest, by attempting a degree of purity impracticable in degenerate times and manners, instead of cutting off the subsisting ill practices, new corruptions might be produced for the concealment and security of the old. It were better, undoubtedly, that no influence at all could affect the mind of a member of Parliament. But of all modes of influence, in my opinion, a place under the government is the least disgraceful to the man who holds it, and by far the most safe to the country. I would not shut out that sort of influence which is open and visible, which is connected with the dignity and the service of the state, when it is not in my power to prevent the influence of contracts, of subscriptions, of direct bribery, and those innumerable methods of clandestine corruption, which are abundantly in the hands of the court, and which will be applied as long as these means of corruption, and the disposition to be corrupted, have existence among us. Our constitution stands on a nice equipoise, with steep precipices and deep waters upon all sides of it. In removing it from a dangerous leaning towards one side, there may be a risk of oversetting it on the other. Every project of a material change in a government so complicated as ours, combined at the same time with external circumstances, still more complicated, is a matter full of difficulties: in which a considerate man will not be too ready to decide; a prudent man too ready to undertake; or an honest man too ready to promise. They do not respect the public nor themselves, who engage for more than they are sure that they ought to attempt, or that they are able to perform. (*Thoughts on the Cause of the Present Discontents*).

BAD TAXES

No man ever doubted that the commodity of tea could bear an imposition of threepence. But no commodity will bear threepence, or will bear a penny, when the general feelings of men are irritated, and two millions of people are resolved not to pay. The feelings of the colonies were formerly the feelings of Great Britain. Theirs were formerly the feelings of Mr. Hampden[8] when called upon for the payment of twenty shillings. Would twenty shillings have ruined Mr. Hampden's fortune?

No! but the payment of half twenty shillings, on the principle it was demanded, would have made him a slave. (Speech on American taxation).

BAD LAWS PRODUCE BASE SUBSERVIENCY, AND MAKE INFORMERS OF CITIZENS

Bad laws are the worst sort of tyranny. In such a country as this they are of all bad things the worst, worse by far than anywhere else; and they derive a particular malignity even from the wisdom and

---

8   John Hampden (1594-1643): An English parliamentarian who opposed "ship money", a tax first imposed to fund emergency coastal defence work, but later it became a general tax.

soundness of the rest of our institutions. For very obvious reasons you cannot trust the crown with a dispensing power over any of your laws. However, a government, be it as bad as it may, will, in the exercise of a discretionary power, discriminate times and persons; and will not ordinarily pursue any man when its own safety is not concerned. A mercenary informer knows no distinction. Under such a system, the obnoxious people are slaves, not only to the government, but they live at the mercy of every individual; they are at once the slaves of the whole community, and of every part of it; and the worst and most unmerciful men are those on whose goodness they most depend.

In this situation men not only shrink from the frowns of a stern magistrate, but they are obliged to fly from their very species. The seeds of destruction are sown in civil intercourse, in social habitudes. The blood of wholesome kindred is infected. Their tables and beds are surrounded with snares. All the means given by Providence to make life safe and comfortable are perverted into instruments of terror and torment. This species of universal subserviency, that makes the very servant who waits behind your chair the arbiter of your life and fortune, has such a tendency to degrade and abase mankind, and to deprive them of that assured and liberal state of mind which alone can make us what we ought to be, that I vow to God I would sooner bring myself to put a man to immediate death for opinions I disliked, and so to get rid of the man and his opinions at once, than to fret him with a feverish being, tainted with the jail-distemper of a contagious servitude, to keep him above ground an animated mass of putrefaction, corrupted himself, and corrupting all about him. (Speech to electors of Bristol).

CANDID POLICY

Refined policy ever has been the parent of confusion; and ever will be so, as long as the world endures. Plain good intention, which is as easily discovered at the first view, as fraud is surely detected at last, is, let me say, of no mean force in the government of mankind.

Genuine simplicity of heart is a healing and cementing principle. (On Conciliation with America).

POLITICS WITHOUT PRINCIPLE

People not very well grounded in the principles of public morality find a set of maxims in office ready made for them, which they assume as naturally and inevitably, as any of the insignia or instruments of the situation. A certain tone of the solid and practical is immediately acquired. Every former profession of public spirit is to be considered as a debauch of youth, or, at best, as a visionary scheme of unattainable perfection. The very idea of consistency is exploded. The convenience of the business of the day is to furnish the principle for doing it. Then the whole ministerial cant is quickly got by heart. The prevalence of faction is to be lamented. All opposition is to be regarded as the effect of envy and disappointed ambition. All administrations are declared to be alike. The same necessity justifies all their measures. It is no longer a matter of discussion, who or what administration is; but that administration is to be supported, is a general maxim. Flattering themselves that their power is become necessary to the support of all order and government, everything which tends to the support of that power is sanctified, and becomes a part of the public interest. (*Observations on a Late State of the Nation*).

VISIONARY POLITICIANS

I have no great opinion of that sublime, abstract, metaphysic reversionary, contingent humanity, which in *cold blood* can subject the *present time* and those who we *daily see and converse with* to immediate calamities in favour of the *future and uncertain* benefit of persons who *only exist in idea*. (Correspondence with A.J.F Dupont.)

THEORIZING POLITICIANS

There are people who have split and anatomised the doctrine of free government, as if it were an abstract question concerning metaphysical liberty and necessity; and not a matter of moral prudence and natural feeling. They have disputed, whether liberty be a positive or a negative idea; whether it does not consist in being governed by laws, without considering what are the laws, or who are the makers; whether man has any rights by nature; and whether all the property he enjoys be not the alms of his government, and his life itself their favour and indulgence.

Others corrupting religion, as these have perverted philosophy, contend, that Christians are redeemed into captivity; and the blood of the Saviour of mankind has been shed to make them the slaves of a few proud and insolent sinners. These shocking extremes provoking to extremes of another kind, speculations are let loose as destructive to all authority, as the former are to all freedom; and every government is called tyranny and usurpation which is not formed on their fancies. In this manner the stirrers-up of this contention, not satisfied with distracting our dependencies[9] and filling them with blood and slaughter, are corrupting our understandings; they are endeavouring

---

[9]   dependencies: children, employees, tenants, apprentices, etc.

to tear up, along with practical liberty, all the foundations of human society, all equity and justice, religion and order. (Letter to the Sheriffs of Bristol).

TRYING TO PLEASE EVERYBODY

The very attempt towards pleasing everybody discovers a temper always flashy, and often false and insincere. Therefore as I have proceeded straight onward in my conduct, so I will proceed in my account of those parts of it which have been most excepted to. But I must first beg leave just to hint to you, that we may suffer very great detriment by being open to every talker. It is not to be imagined how much of service is lost from spirits full of activity and full of energy, who are pressing, who are rushing forward, to great and capital objects, when you oblige them to be continually looking back. Whilst they are defending one service, they defraud you of an hundred. Applaud us when we run; console us when we fall; cheer us when we recover; but let us pass on—for God's sake let us pass on. (Speech to the Bristol electors).

POPULARITY A FALLACIOUS STANDARD

When we know, that the opinions of even the greatest multitudes are the standard of rectitude, I shall think myself obliged to make those opinions the masters of my conscience. But if it may be doubted whether Omnipotence itself is competent to alter the essential constitution of right and wrong, sure I am that such *things*, as they and I, are possessed of no such power. No man carries further than I do the policy of making government pleasing to the people. But the widest range of this politic complaisance is confined within the limits of justice. I would not only consult the interest of the people, but I would cheerfully gratify their humours. We are all a sort of children that must be soothed and managed. I think I am not austere or formal in my nature. I would bear, I would even myself play my part in any innocent buffooneries to divert them. But I never will act the tyrant for their amusement. If they will mix malice in their sports, I shall never consent to throw them any living, sentient creature whatsoever—no, not so much as a kitling, to torment. (Speech to the electors of Bristol).

A SERVILE PARLIAMENT

The House of Commons is not, by its complexion, peculiarly subject to the distempers of an independent habit. Very little compulsion is necessary, on the part of the people, to render it abundantly complaisant to ministers and favourites of all descriptions. It required a great length of time, very considerable industry and perseverance, no vulgar policy, the union of many men and many tempers, and the concurrence of events which do not happen every day, to build up an independent House of Commons. Its demolition was accomplished in a moment; and it was the work of ordinary hands. But to construct is a matter of skill; to demolish, force and fury are sufficient.

The late House of Commons has been punished for its independence. That example is made. Have we an example on record of a House of Commons punished for its servility? The rewards of a senate so disposed are manifest to the world. Several gentlemen are very desirous of altering the constitution of the House of Commons; but they must alter the frame and constitution of human nature itself before they can so fashion it by any mode of election that its conduct will not be influenced by reward and punishment, by fame, and by disgrace. If these examples take root in the minds of men, what members hereafter will be bold enough not to be corrupt? Especially as the king's highway of obsequiousness is so very broad and easy. To make a passive member of parliament, no dignity of mind, no principles of honour, no resolution, no ability, no industry, no learning, no experience, are in the least degree necessary. To defend a post of importance against a powerful enemy, requires an Elliot[10]; a drunken invalid is qualified to hoist a white flag, or to deliver up the keys of the fortress on his knees. (Representation to the King, via Speech to the House).

THE RIGHT PEOPLE FOR THE JOB

We shall never be such fools as to call in an enemy to the substance of any system to remove its corruption, to supply its defects, or to perfect its construction. If our religious tenets should ever want a further elucidation, we shall not call in atheism to explain them. (*Reflections on the Revolution in France*).

THE IMPRACTICABLE UNDESIRABLE

I know it is common for men to say, that such and such things are perfectly right—very desirable; but that, unfortunately, they are not practicable. Oh! no, sir, no. Those things, which are not practicable, are not desirable. There is nothing in the world really beneficial that does not lie within the reach of an informed understanding, and a well-directed pursuit. There is nothing that God has judged good for us that he has not given us the means to accomplish, both in the

---

10 George Elliott (1717-1790), a Scottish officer in the British Army, notable for his determined, brave action in important battles.

natural and the moral world. If we cry, like children, for the moon, like children we must cry on. (Speech to the House on economic reform).

ATTENDANCE TO SPECIFIC REALITIES

I must see with my own eyes, I must, in a manner touch with my own hands, not only the fixed but the momentary circumstances, before I could venture to suggest any political project whatsoever. I must know the power and disposition to accept, to execute, to preserve. I must see the means of correcting the plan, where correctives would be wanted. I must see the things; I must see the men. (Letter to a member of the French National Assembly.)

PRUDENCE OF TIMELY REFORM

I do most seriously put it to administration, to consider the wisdom of a timely reform. Early reformations are amicable arrangements with a friend in power; late reformations are terms imposed upon a conquered enemy: early reformations are made in cool blood; late reformations are made under a state of inflammation. In that state of things people behold in government nothing that is respectable. They see the abuse, and they will see nothing else: they fall into the temper of a furious populace provoked at the disorder of a house of ill-fame; they never attempt to correct or regulate; they go to work by the shortest way—they abate the nuisance, they pull down the house. (Letter to the Sheriffs of Bristol).

DIFFICULTIES OF REFORMERS

Nothing, you know, is more common than for men to wish, and call loudly, too, for a reformation, who, when it arrives, do by no means like the severity of its aspect. Reformation is one of those pieces which must be put at some distance in order to please. Its greatest favourers love it better in the abstract than in the substance. When any old prejudice of their own, or any interest that they value, is touched, they become scrupulous, they become captious, and every man has his separate exception. Some pluck out the black hairs, some the gray; one point must be given up to one; another point must be yielded to another; nothing is suffered to prevail upon its own principle; the whole is so frittered down, and disjointed, that scarcely a trace of the original scheme remains! Thus, between the resistance of power, and the unsystematical process of popularity, the undertaker and the undertaking are both exposed, and the poor reformer is hissed off the stage both by friends and foes. (Speech to the House on Economic Reform).

WISDOM OF CONCESSION

Peace implies reconciliation; and where there has been a material dispute, reconciliation does in a manner always imply concession on the one part or the other. In this state of things I make no difficulty in affirming that the proposal ought to originate from us. Great and acknowledged force is not impaired, either in effect or in opinion, by an unwillingness to exert itself. The superior power may offer peace with honour and with safety. Such an offer from such a power will be attributed to magnanimity. But the concessions of the weak are the concessions of fear. When such a one is disarmed, he is wholly at the mercy of his superior; and he loses for ever that time and those chances which, as they happen to all men, are the strength and resources of all inferior power. (Speech on Conciliation with America).

WISDOM OF COMPROMISE

All government, indeed every human benefit and enjoyment, every virtue, and every prudent act, is founded on compromise and barter. We balance inconveniences; we give and take; we remit some rights, that we may enjoy others; and we choose rather to be happy citizens than subtle disputants. As we must give away some natural liberty, to enjoy civil advantages; so we must sacrifice some civil liberties for the advantages derived from the communion and fellowship of a great empire. But, in all fair dealings, the thing bought must bear some proportion to the purchase paid. None will barter away the immediate jewel of his soul. Though a great house is apt to make slaves haughty, yet it is purchasing a part of the artificial importance of a great empire too dear to pay for it all the essential tights and all the intrinsic dignity of human nature. None of us who would not risk his life rather than fall under a government purely arbitrary. But although there are some amongst us who think our constitution wants many improvements, to make it a complete system of liberty, perhaps none who are of that opinion would think it right to aim at such improvement by disturbing his country, and risking everything that is so dear to him. In every arduous enterprise, we consider what we are to lose as well as what we are to gain; and the more and better stake of liberty every people possess, the less they will hazard in a vain attempt to make it more. These are *the cords of man*. Man acts from adequate motives relative to his interest; and not on metaphysical speculations. Aristotle, the great master of reasoning, cautions us, and with great weight and propriety, against this species of delusive geometrical accuracy in moral arguments, as the most fallacious of all sophistry. (Speech on Conciliation with the Colonies).

FALLACY OF EXTREMES

It is a fallacy in constant use with those who would level all things, and confound right with wrong, to insist upon the inconveniences which are attached to every choice, without taking into consideration the different weight and consequence of those inconveniences. The question is not concerning *absolute* discontent or *perfect* satisfaction in government; neither of which can be pure and unmixed at any time, or upon any system. The controversy is about that degree of good humour in the people, which may possibly be attained, and ought certainly to be looked for. While some politicians may be waiting to know whether the sense of every individual be against them, accurately distinguishing the vulgar from the better sort, drawing lines between the enterprises of a faction and the efforts of a people, they may chance to see the government, which they are so nicely weighing, and dividing, and distinguishing, tumble to the ground in the midst of their wise deliberation. Prudent men, when so great an object as the security of government, or even its peace, is at stake, will not run the risk of a decision which may be fatal to it. They who can read the political sky will see a hurricane in a cloud no bigger than a hand at the very edge of the horizon, and will run into the first harbour. No lines can be laid down for civil or political wisdom. They are a matter incapable of exact definition. But, though no man can draw a stroke between the confines of day and night, yet light and darkness are, upon the whole, tolerably distinguishable. Nor will it be impossible for a prince to find out such a mode of government, and such persons to administer it, as will give a great degree of content to his people; without any curious and anxious research for that abstract, universal, perfect harmony, which, while he is seeking, he abandons those means of ordinary tranquillity which are in his power without any research at all. (*Thoughts on the Cause of the Present Discontents*).

THE LIMITS OF FORCE

America, gentlemen say, is a noble object. It is an object well worth fighting for. Certainly it is, if fighting a people be the best way of gaining them. Gentlemen in this respect will be led to their choice of means by their complexions and their habits. Those who understand the military art will of course have some predilection for it. Those who wield the thunder of the state may have more confidence in the efficacy of arms. But I confess, possibly for want of this knowledge, my opinion is much more in favour of prudent management, than of force; considering force not as an odious, but a feeble instrument for preserving a people so numerous, so active, so growing, as spirited as this, in a profitable and subordinate connexion with us.

First, Sir, permit me to observe that the use of force alone is *temporary*. It may subdue for a moment; but it does not remove the necessity of subduing again: and a nation is not governed which is perpetually to be conquered.

My next objection is its *uncertainty*. Terror is not always the effect of force; and an armament is not a victory. If you do not succeed, you are without resource; for, conciliation failing, force remains; but, force failing, no further hope of reconciliation is left. Power and authority are sometimes bought by kindness; but they can never be begged as alms by an impoverished and defeated violence.

A further objection to force is that you *impair the object* by your very efforts to preserve it. The things you fought for is not the thing which you recover; but depreciated, sunk, wasted, and consumed in the contest. Nothing less will content me than *whole America*. I do not choose to consume its strength along with our own; because in all parts it is the British strength that I consume. I do not choose to be caught by a foreign enemy at the end of this exhausting conflict; and still less in the midst of it. I may escape; but I make no insurance against such an event. Let me add that I do not choose to break the American spirit; because it is the spirit that has made the country.

Lastly, we have no experience in favour of force as an instrument in the rule of our colonies. Their growth and their utility has been owing to a method altogether different. Our ancient indulgence has been said to be pursued to a fault. It may be so. But we know, if feeling is evidence, that our fault was more tolerable than our attempt to mend it; and our sin far more salutary than our penitence. (Speech on Conciliation with the Colonies).

CARELESS CALLS FOR VIOLENCE

A conscientious man would be cautious how he dealt in blood. He would feel some apprehension at being called to a tremendous account for engaging in so deep a play, without any sort of knowledge of the game. It is no excuse for presumptuous ignorance, that it is directed by insolent passion. The poorest being that crawls on earth, contending to save itself from injustice and oppression, is an object respectable in the eyes of God and man. But I cannot conceive any existence under heaven (which, in the depths of its wisdom, tolerates all sorts of things) that is more truly odious and disgusting, than an impotent helpless creature, without civil wisdom or military skill, without a consciousness of any other qualification for power but his servility to it, bloated with pride and arrogance, calling for battles which he is not to fight, contending for a violent dominion which he can never exercise, and satisfied to be himself mean and miserable, in order to render others contemptible and wretched. (Letter to the Sheriffs of Bristol).

WAR IS NO EXPERIMENT

As if war was a matter of experiment! As if you could take it up or lay it down as an idle frolic! As if the dire goddess that presides over it, with her murderous spear in hand, and her gorgon at her breast, was a coquette to be flirted with! We ought with reverence to approach that tremendous divinity, that loves courage, but commands counsel. War never leaves where it found a nation. It is never to be entered into without mature deliberation; not a deliberation lengthened out into a perplexing indecision, but a deliberation leading to a sure and fixed judgment. When so taken up, it is not to be abandoned without reason as valid, as fully, and as extensively considered. Peace may be made as unadvisedly as war. Nothing is so rash as fear; and the councils of pusillanimity very rarely put off, whilst they are always sure to aggravate, the evils from which they would fly.

In that great war carried on against Louis the Fourteenth, for near eighteen years, Government spared no pains to satisfy the nation that, though they were to be animated by a desire of glory, glory was not their ultimate object; but that every thing dear to them, in religion, in law, in liberty—every thing which as freemen, as Englishmen, and as citizens of the great commonwealth of Christendom, they had at heart, was then at stake. This was to know the true art of gaining the affections and confidence of an high-minded people; this was to understand human nature. A danger to avert a danger; a present inconvenience and suffering to prevent a foreseen future, and a worse calamity; these are the motives that belong to an animal, who, in his constitution, is at once adventurous and provident; circumspect and daring; whom his Creator has made, as the Poet[11] says, "of large discourse, looking before and after." But never can a vehement and sustained spirit of fortitude be kindled in a people by a war of calculation. It has nothing that can keep the mind erect under the gusts of adversity. Even where men are willing, as sometimes they are, to barter their blood for lucre, to hazard their safety for the gratification of their avarice, the passion which animates them to that sort of conflict, like all the short-sighted passions, must see it's objects distinct and near at hand. The passions of the lower order are hungry and impatient. Speculative plunder; contingent spoil; future, long adjourned, uncertain booty; pillage which must enrich a late posterity, and which possibly may not reach to posterity at all; these, for any length of time, will never support a mercenary war. The people are in the right. The calculation of profit in all such wars is false. On balancing the account of such wars, ten thousand hogsheads of sugar are purchased at ten thousand times their price. The blood of man should never be shed but to redeem the blood of man. It is well shed for our family, for our friends, for our God, for our country, for our kind. The rest is vanity; the rest is crime. (*Letters on a Regicide Peace*).

---

11 Shakespeare, with the following quote from *Hamlet*.

2

MORAL PHILOSOPHY

JUDGING YOUR LOCAL REPRESENTATIVE.

Look, gentlemen, to the *whole tenor* of your member's conduct. Try whether his ambition or his avarice have jostled him out of the straight line of duty; or whether that grand foe of the offices of active life, that master vice in men of business, a degenerate and inglorious sloth—has made him flag and languish in his course. This is the object of our inquiry. If our member's conduct can bear this touch, mark it for sterling. He may have fallen into errors; he must have faults; but our error is greater, and our fault is radically ruinous to ourselves, if we do not bear, if we do not even applaud, the whole compound and mixed mass of such a character. Not to act thus is folly; I had almost said it is impiety. He censures God, who quarrels with the imperfections of man...

Let me say with plainness, I who am no longer in a public character[12],

---

12 Burke was at this time out of the House of Commons. His service there was not wholly continuous.

that if by a fair, by an indulgent, by a gentlemanly behaviour to our representatives, we do not give confidence to their minds, and a liberal scope to their understandings; if we do not permit our members to act upon a *very* enlarged view of things; we shall at length infallibly degrade our national representation into a confused and scuffling bustle of local agency. When the popular member is narrowed in his ideas, and rendered timid in his proceedings, the service of the crown will be the sole nursery of statesmen. Among the frolics of the court, it may at length take that of attending to its business. Then the monopoly of mental power will be added to the power of all other kinds it possesses. On the side of the people there will be nothing but impotence: for ignorance is impotence; narrowness of mind is impotence; timidity is itself impotence, and makes all other qualities that go along with it, impotent and useless. (Speech to the Bristol electors).

MODESTY OF MIND

If any inquiry thus carefully conducted should fail at last of discovering the truth, it may answer an end perhaps as useful, in discovering to us the weakness of our own understanding. If it does not make us knowing, it may make us modest. If it does not preserve us from error, it may at least from the spirit of error; and may make us cautious of pronouncing with positiveness or with haste, when so much labour may end in so much uncertainty. (*A Philosophical Enquiry into the Origin of Our Ideas of the Sublime and Beautiful*).

HUMAN LIMITATIONS

Individuals are physical beings, subject to laws universal and invariable. The immediate cause acting in these laws may be obscure: the general results are subject of certain calculation. But commonwealths are not physical, but moral essences. They are artificial combinations, and, in their proximate efficient cause, the arbitrary productions of the human mind. We are not yet acquainted with the laws which necessarily influence the stability of that kind of agent. There is not in the physical order (with which they do not appear to hold any assignable connection) a distinct cause by which any of those fabrics must necessarily grow, flourish, or decay; nor, in my opinion, does the moral world produce anything more determinate on that subject than what may serve as an amusement (liberal, indeed, and ingenious, but still only an amusement) for speculative men. I doubt whether the history of mankind is yet complete enough, if ever it can be so, to furnish grounds for a sure theory on the internal causes which necessarily affect the fortune of a state. I am far from denying the operation of such causes; but they are infinitely uncertain and much more obscure, and much more difficult to trace, than the foreign causes that tend to raise, to depress and sometimes to overwhelm a community. (*Letters on a Regicide Peace.*)

ALL PEOPLE ARE SUBJECTS

We have no arbitrary power to give, because arbitrary power is a thing which neither any man can hold nor any man can give. No man can lawfully govern himself according to his own will, much less can one person be governed by the will of another. We are all born in subjection, all born equally, high and low, governors and governed, in subjection to one great, immutable, pre-existent law, prior to all our devices, and prior to all our contrivances, paramount to all our ideas and all our sensations, antecedent to our very existence, by which we are knit and connected in the eternal frame of the universe, out of which we cannot stir.

This great law does not arise from our conventions or compacts; on the contrary, it gives to our conventions and compacts all the force and sanction that they have;— it does not arise from our vain institutions. Every good gift is of God[13]; all power is of God;— and He, who has given the power, and from whom alone it originates, will never suffer the exercise of it to be practised upon any less solid foundation than the power itself. If then all dominion over man over man is the effect of the Divine disposition, it is bound by the eternal laws of Him who gave it, with which no human authority can dispense; neither he that exercises it, nor even those who are subject to it; and, if they were made enough to make an express compact that should release their magistrate from his duty, and should declare their lives, their liberties, and properties dependent upon, not rules and laws, but his mere capricious will, that covenant would be void. The accepter of it has not his authority increased, but he has his crime doubled. Therefore can it be imagined, if this be true, that He will suffer this great gift of government, the greatest, the best that was ever given by God to mankind, to be the plaything and the sport of the feeble will of man, who by a blasphemous, absurd, and petulant usurpation, would place his own feeble, contemptible, ridiculous will in the place of the Divine wisdom and justice? (From the Speech on the Impeachment of Warren Hastings[14]).

---

13 Epistle of James 1:17.

14 Warren Hastings was Governor-General of British India. Burke considered his governorship, too closely linked with greedy mercantile interests, a scandal during a time of turmoil, drought and widespread hunger. Hastings was acquitted after a 7 year investigation.

CIVIL FREEDOM.

Civil freedom, gentlemen, is not, as many have endeavoured to persuade you, a thing that lies hid in the depth of abstruse science. It is a blessing and a benefit, not an abstract speculation; and all the just reasoning that can be upon it is of so coarse a texture, as perfectly to suit the ordinary capacities of those who are to enjoy, and of those who are to defend it. Far from any resemblance to those propositions in geometry and metaphysics, which admit no medium, but must be true or false in all their latitude; social and civil freedom, like all other things in common life, are variously mixed and modified, enjoyed in very different degrees, and shaped into an infinite diversity of forms, according to the temper and circumstances of every community. The *extreme* of liberty (which is its abstract perfection, but its real fault) obtains nowhere, nor ought to obtain anywhere. Because extremes, as we all know, in every point which relates either to our duties or satisfactions in life, are destructive both to virtue and enjoyment. (Letter to the Sheriffs of Bristol).

RATIONAL LIBERTY.

Liberty, too, must be limited in order to be possessed. The degree of restraint it is impossible in any case to settle precisely. But it ought to be the constant aim of every wise public council to find out by cautious experiments, and rational, cool endeavours, with how little, not how much, of this restraint the community can subsist. For liberty is a good to be improved, and not an evil to be lessened. It is not only a private blessing of the first order, but the vital spring and energy of the state itself, which has just so much life and vigour as there is liberty in it. But whether liberty be advantageous or not (for I know it is a fashion to decry the very principle), none will dispute that peace is a blessing; and peace must in the course of human affairs be frequently bought by some indulgence and toleration at least to liberty. For as the sabbath (though of Divine institution) was made for man, not man for the sabbath, government, which can claim no higher origin or authority, in its exercise at least, ought to conform to the exigencies of the time, and the temper and character of the people with whom it is concerned; and not always to attempt violently to bend the people to their theories of subjection. The bulk of mankind on their part are not excessively curious concerning any theories whilst they are really happy; and one sure symptom of an ill-conducted state is the propensity of the people to resort to them. (Letter To The Sheriffs Of Bristol).

WHEN IS CIVIL DISOBEDIENCE JUSTIFIED?

The speculative line of demarcation, where obedience ought to end and resistance must begin, is faint, obscure and not easily definable. It is not a single act, or a single event, which determines it. Governments must be abused and deranged indeed, before it can be thought of; and the prospect of the future must be as bad as the experience of the past. When things are in that lamentable condition, the nature of the disease is to indicate the remedy to those whom nature has qualified to administer in extremities this critical, ambiguous, bitter potion to a distempered state. Times, and occasions, and provocations will teach their own lessons. The wise will determine from the gravity of the case; the irritable, from sensibility to oppression, the high-minded, from disdain and indignation at abusive power in unworthy hands; the brave and bold, from the love of honourable danger in a generous cause: but, with or without right, a revolution will be the very last resource of the thinking and the good. (*Reflections on the Revolution in France*).

CULTURE, NOT CONTRACTS, UNITE PEOPLE.

We lay too much weight upon the formality of treaties and compacts. We do not act much more wisely when we trust to the interests of men as guarantees of their engagements. The interest frequently tear to pieces the engagements; and the passions trample upon both. Entirely to trust to either, is to disregard our own safety, or not to know mankind. Men are not tied to one another by papers and seals. They are led to associate by resemblances, by conformities, by sympathies. It is with a nation as with individuals. Nothing is so strong a tie of amity between nation and nation as correspondence in laws, customs, manners, and habits of life. They have more than the force of treaties in themselves. They are obligations written in the heart. They approximate men to men, without their knowledge, and sometimes against their intentions. The secret, unseen, but irrefragable bond of habitual intercourse holds them together, even when their perverse and litigious nature sets them to equivocate, scuffle, and fight, about the terms of their written obligations. (*Letters to a Regicide Prince*).

DUTY NOT BASED ON WILL.

I cannot too often recommend it to the serious consideration of all men, who think civil society to be within the province of moral jurisdiction, that if we owe to it any duty, it is not subject to our will. Duties are not voluntary. Duty and will are even contradictory terms. Now, though civil society might be at first a voluntary act (which in many cases it undoubtedly was), its continuance is under a permanent, standing covenant, co-existing with the society; and it attaches upon every individual of that society, without any formal act of his own. This is warranted by the general practice, arising out of the general sense of mankind. Men without their choice derive benefits from that association; without their choice they are subjected to duties in consequence of these benefits; and without their choice they enter into a virtual obligation as binding as any that is actual. Look through the whole of life and the whole system of duties. Much the strongest moral obligations are such as were never the results of our option. I allow, that if no supreme ruler exists, wise to form, and potent to enforce, the moral law, there is no sanction to any contract, virtual or even actual, against the will of prevalent power. On that hypothesis, let any set of men be strong enough to set their duties at defiance, and they cease to be duties any longer. We have but this one appeal against irresistible power—

> "*Si genus humanum et mortalia temnitis arma,*
>   *At sperate Deos memores fandi atque nefandi*[15]."

Taking it for granted that I do not write to the disciples of the Parisian philosophy[16], I may assume, that the awful Author of our being is the Author of our place in the order of existence; and that, having disposed and marshalled us by a divine tactic, not according to our will, but according to his, he has, in and by that disposition, virtually subjected us to act the part which belongs to the place assigned us. We have obligations to mankind at large, which are not in consequence of any special voluntary pact. They arise from the relation of man to man, and the relation of man to God, which relations are not matters of choice. On the contrary, the force of all the pacts which we enter into with any particular person, or number of persons, amongst mankind, depends upon those prior obligations. In some cases the subordinate

---

15 Virgil, *The Aeneid*. Latin: You who despise humanity and the rules of arms, remember: the Gods keep count of your transgressions.

16 Parisian philosophy: French philosophers who inspired the tenets expressed in the 1789 revolution.

relations are voluntary, in others they are necessary—but the duties are all compulsive. When we marry, the choice is voluntary, but the duties are not matter of choice. They are dictated by the nature of the situation. Dark and inscrutable are the ways by which we come into the world. The instincts which give rise to this mysterious process of nature are not of our making. But out of physical causes, unknown to us, perhaps unknowable, arise moral duties, which, as we are able perfectly to comprehend, we are bound indispensably to perform. Parents may not be consenting to their moral relation; but consenting or not, they are bound to a long train of burthensome duties towards those with whom they have never made a convention of any sort. Children are not consenting to their relation, but their relation, without their actual consent, binds them to its duties; or rather it implies their consent, because the presumed consent of every rational creature is in unison with the predisposed order of things. Men come in that manner into a community with the social state of their parents, endowed with all the benefits, loaded with all the duties, of their situation. If the social ties and ligaments, spun out of those physical relations which are the elements of the commonwealth, in most cases begin, and alway continue, independently of our will, so, without any stipulation on our own part, are we bound by that relation called our country, which comprehends (as it has been well said) "all the charities of all." Nor are we left without powerful instincts to make this duty as dear and grateful to us, as it is awful and coercive. It consists, in a great measure, in the ancient order into which we are born. We may have the same geographical situation, but another country; as we may have the same country in another soil. The place that determines our duty to our country is a social, civil relation. (*An Appeal from the New to the Old Whigs*).

PRUDENCE

Prudence (in all things a Virtue, in Politicks the first of Virtues)....
Believe me, Sir, in all changes in the State, Moderation is a Virtue, not
only amiable but powerful. It is a disposing, arranging, conciliating,
cementing Virtue ... To dare to be fearful when all about you are full
of presumption and confidence... (Letter to C. de Pont.)

LONG-LASTING PREJUDICES ARE VALUABLE

You see, Sir, that in this enlightened age I am bold enough to confess
that we are generally men of untaught feelings; that, instead of casting
away all our old prejudices, we cherish them to a very considerable
degree and, to take more shame to ourselves, we cherish them because
they are prejudices; and the longer they have lasted and the more
generally they have prevailed, the more we cherish them. We are
afraid to put men to live and trade each on his own private stock
of reason; because we suspect that the stock in each man is small,
and that the individuals would do better to avail themselves of the
general bank and capital of nations and of ages. Many of our men
of speculation, instead of exploding general prejudices, employ their
sagacity to discover the latent wisdom which prevails in them. If they
find what they seek, and they seldom fail, they think it more wise to
continue the prejudice, with the reason involved, than to cast away the
coat of prejudice, and to leave nothing but the naked reason; because
prejudice, with its reason, has a motive to give action to that reason,
and an affection which will give it permanence. Prejudice is of ready
application in the emergency; it previously engages the mind in a steady
course of wisdom and virtue, and does not leave a man hesitating in a
the moment of decision, sceptical, puzzled, and unresolved. Prejudice
renders a man's virtue his habit; and not a series of unconnected acts.

Through just prejudice, his duty becomes part of his nature. (*Reflections on the Revolution in France*).

ENGLISH CONSERVATION AND CORRECTION

A state without the means of some change is without the means of its conservation. Without such means it might even risk the loss of that part of the constitution which it wished the most religiously to preserve. The two principles of conservation and correction operated strongly at the two critical periods of the Restoration[17] and Revolution, when England found itself without a king. At both those periods the nation had lost the bond of union in their ancient edifice; they did not, however, dissolve the whole fabric. On the contrary, in both cases they regenerated the deficient part of the old constitution through the parts which were not impaired. They kept these old parts exactly as they were, that the part recovered might be suited to them. They acted by the ancient organized states in the shape of their old organization, and not by the organic molecule of a disbanded people. At no time, perhaps, did the sovereign legislature manifest a more tender regard to that fundamental principle of British constitutional policy than at the time of the Revolution, when it deviated from the direct line of hereditary succession. The crown was carried somewhat out of the line in which it had before moved; but the new line was derived from the same stock. It was still a line of hereditary descent; still an hereditary descent in the same blood, though an hereditary descent qualified with Protestantism. When the legislature altered the direction, but kept the principle, they showed that they held it inviolable. (*Reflections on the Revolution in France*).

---

17 Restoration: In 1660 King Charles II gained the thrown after an unstable period in the British isles, including an English dalliance with republicanism under Oliver Cromwell.

NATURE'S GENEROUS PROVISION

If honesty be true policy with regard to the transient interest of individuals, it is much more certainly so with regard to the permanent interest of communities. I know that it is but too natural for us to see our own *certain* ruin in the possible *prosperity* of other people. It is hard to persuade us that everything which is *got* by another is not *taken* from ourselves. But it is fit that we should get the better of these suggestions, which come from what is not the best and soundest part of our nature, and that we should form to ourselves a way of thinking more rational, more just, and more religious. Trade is not a limited thing; as if the objects of mutual demand and consumption could not stretch beyond the bounds of our jealousies. God has given the earth to the children of men, and He has undoubtedly, in giving it to them, given them what is abundantly sufficient for all their exigencies; not a scanty, but a most liberal provision for them all. The Author of our nature has written it strongly in that nature, and has promulgated the same law in His written word, that man shall eat his bread by his labour; and I am persuaded that no man, and no combination of men, for their own ideas of particular profit, can, without great impiety, undertake to say that he *shall not* do so; that they have no sort of right either to prevent the labour or to withhold the bread. (Two Letters to Gentlemen in the City of Bristol).

NATURE ANTICIPATES MAN.

Whenever the wisdom of our Creator intended that we should be affected with anything, he did not confide the execution of his design to the languid and precarious operation of our reason; but he endued it with powers and properties that prevent the understanding, and even the will; which, seizing upon the senses and imagination, captivate the soul before the understanding is ready either to join with them, or to oppose them. It is by a long deduction, and much study, that we discover the adorable wisdom of God in his works: when we discover it, the effect is very different, not only in the manner of acquiring it, but in its own nature, from that which strikes us without any preparation from the sublime or the beautiful. (*A Philosophical Enquiry into the Origin of Our Ideas of the Sublime and Beautiful*).

THEORY AND PRACTICE

It is, I own, not uncommon to be wrong in theory, and right in practice; and we are happy that it is so. Men often act right from their feelings, who afterwards reason but ill on them from principle: but as it is impossible to avoid an attempt at such reasoning, and equally impossible to prevent its having some influence on our practice, surely it is worth taking some pains to have it just, and founded on the basis of sure experience. (*A Philosophical Enquiry into the Origin of Our Ideas of the Sublime and Beautiful*).

INDUCTION AND COMPARISON

We must not attempt to fly, when we can scarcely pretend to creep. In considering any complex matter, we ought to examine every distinct ingredient in the composition, one by one; and reduce everything to the utmost simplicity; since the condition of our nature binds us to a strict law and vary narrow limits. We ought afterwards to re-examine the principles by the effect of the composition, as well as the composition by that of the principles. We ought to compare our subject with things of a similar nature, and even with things of a contrary nature; for discoveries may be, and often are, made by the contrast, which would escape us on the single view. The greater number of the comparisons we make, the more general and the more certain our knowledge is likely to prove, as built upon a more extensive and perfect induction. (*A Philosophical Enquiry into the Origin of Our Ideas of the Sublime and Beautiful*).

THE LIMITS OF SCIENCE.

When Newton first discovered the property of attraction, and settled its laws[18], he found it served very well to explain several of the most remarkable phenomena in nature; but yet with reference to the general system of things, he could consider attraction but as an effect, whose cause at that time he did not attempt to trace. But when he afterwards began to account for it by a subtle elastic aether, this great man (if in so great a man it be not impious to discover anything like a blemish) seemed to have quitted his usual cautious manner of philosophising: since, perhaps, allowing all that has been advanced on this subject to be sufficiently proved, I think it leaves us with as many difficulties as it found us. That great chain of causes, which linking one to another even to the throne of God himself, can never be unravelled by any industry of ours. When we go but one step beyond the immediate sensible qualities of things, we go out of our depth. All we do after is but a faint struggle, that shows we are in an element which does not belong to us. (*A Philosophical Enquiry into the Origin of our Ideas Of the Sublime and Beautiful*).

---

18 Sir Isaac Newton (1642-1735), perhaps England's most famous scientist, published his *Mathematical Principles of Natural Philosophy* in 1687, establishing the laws of gravitation and motion.

The nature of things is, I admit, a sturdy adversary. (*Letters on a Regicide Peace.*)

INVESTIGATION.

I am convinced that the method of teaching which approaches most nearly to the method of investigation is incomparably the best; since, not content with serving up a few barren and lifeless truths, it leads to the stock on which they grew; it tends to set the reader himself in the track of invention, and to direct him into those paths in which the author has made his own discoveries, if he should be so happy as to have made any that are valuable. (*A Philosophical Enquiry into the Origin of our Ideas Of the Sublime and Beautiful*).

USE OF THEORY.

A theory founded on experiment, and not assumed, is always good for so much as it explains. Our inability to push it indefinitely is no argument at all against it. This inability may be owing to our ignorance of some necessary mediums; to a want of proper application; to many other causes besides a defect in the principles we employ. (*A Philosophical Enquiry into the Origin of our Ideas Of the Sublime and Beautiful*).

BONDS OF SYMPATHY.

Whenever we are formed by nature to any active purpose, the passion which animates us to it is attended with delight, or a pleasure of some kind, let the subject-matter be what it will; and as our Creator had designed that we should be united by the bond of sympathy, he has strengthened that bond by a proportionable delight; and there most where our sympathy is most wanted,—in the distresses of others. (*A Philosophical Enquiry into the Origin of Our Ideas of the Sublime and Beautiful*).

For sympathy must be considered as a sort of substitution, by which we are put into the place of another man, and affected in many respects as he is affected; so that this passion may either partake of the nature of those which regard self-preservation, and turning upon pain may be a source of the sublime; or it may turn upon ideas of pleasure; and then whatever has been said of the social affections, whether they regard society in general, or only some particular modes of it, may be applicable here. It is by this principle chiefly that poetry, painting, and other affecting arts, transfuse their passions from one breast to another, and are often capable of grafting a delight on wretchedness, misery, and death itself. (*A Philosophical Enquiry into the Origin of Our Ideas of the Sublime and Beautiful*).

IMITATION AN INSTINCTIVE LAW.

For as sympathy makes us take a concern in whatever men feel, so this affection prompts us to copy whatever they do; and consequently we have a pleasure in imitating, and in whatever belongs to imitation merely as it is such, without any intervention of the reasoning faculty, but solely from our natural constitution, which Providence has framed in such a manner as to find either pleasure or delight, according to the nature of the object, in whatever regards the purposes of our being. It is by imitation far more than by precept, that we learn everything; and what we learn thus, we acquire not only more effectually, but more pleasantly. This forms our manners, our opinions, our lives. It is one of the strongest links of society; it is a species of mutual compliance, which all men yield to each other, without constraint to themselves, and which is extremely flattering to all. (*A Philosophical Enquiry into the Origin of our Ideas Of the Sublime and Beautiful*).

STANDARD OF REASON AND TASTE.

It is probable that the standard both of reason and taste is the same in all human creatures. For if there were not some principles of judgment as well as of sentiment common to all mankind, no hold could possibly be taken either on their reason or their passions, sufficient to maintain the ordinary correspondence of life. (*A Philosophical Enquiry into the Origin of our Ideas Of the Sublime and Beautiful*).

BEAUTY AND AFFECTION.

The object therefore of this mixed passion, which we call love, is the *beauty* of the sex. Men are carried to the sex in general, as it is the sex, and by the common law of nature; but they are attached to particulars by personal *beauty*. I call beauty a social quality; for where women and men, and not only they, but when other animals give us a sense of joy and pleasure in beholding them (and there are many that do so), they inspire us with sentiments of tenderness and affection towards their persons; we like to have them near us, and we enter willingly into a kind of relation with them, unless we should have strong reasons to the contrary. (*A Philosophical Enquiry into the Origin of Our Ideas of the Sublime and Beautiful*).

SELF-INSPECTION

Whatever turns the soul inward on itself, tends to concentre its forces, and to fit it for greater and stronger flights of science. By looking into physical causes our minds are opened and enlarged; and in this pursuit, whether we take or whether we lose our game, the chase is certainly of service. (*A Philosophical Enquiry into the Origin of Our Ideas of the Sublime and Beautiful*).

AMBITION AND COMPLACENCY

God has planted in man a sense of ambition, and a satisfaction arising from the contemplation of his excelling his fellows in something deemed valuable amongst them. It is this passion that drives men to all the ways we see in use of signalizing themselves, and that tends to make whatever excites in a man the idea of this distinction so very pleasant. It has been so strong as to make very miserable men take comfort, that they were supreme in misery; and certain it is, that, where we cannot distinguish ourselves by something excellent, we begin to take a complacency in some singular infirmities, follies, or defects of one kind or other. It is on this principle that flattery is so prevalent; for flattery is no more than what raises in a man's mind an idea of a preference which he has not. (*A Philosophical Enquiry into the Origin of Our Ideas of the Sublime and Beautiful*).

POWER OF WORDS

Natural objects affect us, by the laws of that connexion which Providence has established between certain motions and configurations of bodies, and certain consequent feelings in our mind. Painting affects in the same manner, but with the superadded pleasure of imitation. Architecture affects by the laws of nature, and the law of reason; from which latter result the rules of proportion, which make a work to be praised or censured, in the whole or in some part, when the end for which it was designed is or is not properly answered. But as to words; they seem to me to affect us in a manner very different from that in which we are affected by natural objects, or by painting or architecture; yet words have as considerable a share in exciting ideas of beauty and of the sublime as many of those, and sometimes a much greater than any of them. (*A Philosophical Enquiry into the Origin of Our Ideas of the Sublime and Beautiful*).

POWER OF THE OBSCURE

Poetry, with all its obscurity, has a more general, as well as a more powerful, dominion over the passions, than the other art. And I think there are reasons in nature, why the obscure idea, when properly conveyed, should be more affecting than the clear. It is our ignorance of things make the most striking causes affect but little. It is thus with the vulgar; and all men are as the vulgar in what they do not understand. The ideas of eternity and infinity, are among the most affecting we have: and yet perhaps there is nothing of which we really understand so little, as of infinity and eternity. (*A Philosophical Enquiry into the Origin of Our Ideas of the Sublime and Beautiful*).

INJUSTICE TO OUR OWN AGE.

If these evil dispositions should spread much farther they must end in our destruction; for nothing can save a people destitute of public and private faith. However, the author, for the present state of things, has extended the charge by much too widely; as men are but too apt to take the measure of all mankind from their own particular acquaintance. Barren as this age may be in the growth of honour and virtue, the country does not want, at this moment, as strong, and those not a few, examples as were ever known, of an unshaken adherence to principle, and attachment to connexion, against every allurement of interest. Those examples are not furnished by the great alone; nor by those, whose activity in public affairs may render it suspected that they make such a character one of the rounds in their ladder of ambition; but by men more quiet, and more in the shade, on whom an unmixed sense of honour alone could operate. (*Observations on a Late State of the Nation*).

NOT AS BAD AS WE SEEM.

Our circumstances are indeed critical; but then they are the critical circumstances of a strong and mighty nation. If corruption and meanness are greatly spread, they are not spread universally. Many public men are hitherto examples of public spirit and integrity. Whole parties, as far as large bodies can be uniform, have preserved character. However they may be deceived in some particulars, I know of no set of men amongst us which does not contain persons on whom the nation, in a difficult exigence, may well value itself. Private life, which is the nursery of the commonwealth, is yet in general pure, and on the whole disposed to virtue; and the people at large want neither generosity nor spirit... What we want is to establish more fully an opinion of uniformity, and consistency of character, in the leading men of the state; such as will restore some confidence to profession and appearance, such as will fix subordination upon esteem. Without this all schemes are begun at the wrong end. (*Observations on a Late State of the Nation*).

LIBELLERS OF HUMAN NATURE.

I hope there are none of you corrupted with the doctrine taught by wicked men for the worst purposes, and received by the malignant credulity of envy and ignorance, which is, that the men who act upon the public stage are all alike; all equally corrupt; all influenced by no other views than the sordid lure of salary and pension. The thing I know by experience to be false. Never expecting to find perfection in men, and not looking for divine attributes in created beings, in my commerce with my contemporaries, I have found much human virtue. I have seen not a little public spirit; a real subordination of interest to duty; and a decent and regulated sensibility to honest fame and reputation. The age unquestionably produces (whether in a greater or less number than former times, I know not) daring profligates, and insidious hypocrites. What then? Am I not to avail myself of whatever good is to be found in the world, because of the mixture of evil that will always be in it? The smallness of the quantity in currency only heightens the value. They who raise suspicions on the good on account of the behaviour of ill men, are of the party of the latter. The common cant is no justification for taking this party. I have been deceived, say they, by Titius and Maevius[19]; I have been the dupe

---

19 Titius and Maevius, Ancient Roman figures: Titius was accused of murder; Maevius was his (ineffective) defence lawyer.

of this pretender or of that mountebank; and I can trust appearances no longer. But my credulity and want of discernment cannot, as I conceive, amount to a fair presumption against any man's integrity. A conscientious person would rather doubt his own judgment, than condemn his species. He would say, I have observed without attention, or judged upon erroneous maxims; I trusted to profession, when I ought to have attended to conduct. Such a man will grow wise, not malignant, by his acquaintance with the world. But he that accuses all mankind of corruption, ought to remember that he is sure to convict only one. In truth I should much rather admit those, whom at any time I have disrelished the most, to be patterns of perfection, than seek a consolation to my own unworthiness, in a general communion of depravity with all about me. (Letter to Sheriffs of Bristol on affairs in America).

A CHARITABLE VIEW

Honest men will not forget either their merit or their sufferings. There are men (and many, I trust, there are) who, out of love to their country and their kind, would torture their invention to find excuses for the mistakes of their brethren; and who, to stifle dissension, would construe even doubtful appearances with the utmost favour: such men will never persuade themselves to be ingenious and refined in discovering disaffection and treason in the manifest, palpable signs of suffering loyalty. Persecution is so unnatural to them, that they gladly snatch the very first opportunity of laying aside all the tricks and devices of penal politics; and of returning home, after all their irksome and vexatious wanderings, to our natural family mansion, to the grand social principle, that unites all men, in all descriptions, under the shadow of an equal and impartial justice. (Speech to the Bristol electors).

FOND CRITICISM

Those who are least anxious about your conduct are not those that love you most. Moderate affection and satiated enjoyment are cold and respectful; but an ardent and injured passion is tempered up with wrath, and grief, and shame, and conscious worth, and the maddening sense of violated right. A jealous love lights his torch from the firebrands of the furies. They who call upon you to belong *wholly* to the people, are those who wish you to return to your *proper* home; to the sphere of your duty, to the post of your honour, to the mansion-house of all genuine, serene, and solid satisfaction. (Speech to the House on economic reform).

LIBERTY AND GENERAL CORRUPTION

This moral levelling is a *servile principle*. It leads to practical passive obedience far better than all the doctrines which the pliant accommodation of theology to power has ever produced. It cuts up by the roots, not only all idea of forcible resistance, but even of civil opposition. It disposes men to an abject submission, not by opinion, which may be shaken by argument or altered by passion, but by the strong ties of public and private interest. For if all men who act in a public situation are equally selfish, corrupt, and venal, what reason can be given for desiring any sort of change, which, besides the evils which must attend all changes, can be productive of no possible advantage? The active men in the state are true samples of the mass. If they are universally depraved, the commonwealth itself is not sound. We may amuse ourselves with talking as much as we please of the virtue of middle or humble life; that is, we may place our confidence in the virtue of those who have never been tried. But if the persons who are continually emerging out of that sphere be no better than those whom birth has placed above it, what hopes are there in the remainder of the body, which is to furnish the perpetual succession of the state? All who have ever written on government are unanimous, that among a people generally corrupt, liberty cannot long exist. And indeed how is it possible? When those who are to make the laws, to guard, to enforce, or to obey them, are, by a tacit confederacy of manners, indisposed to the spirit of all generous and noble institutions. (Speech after the election of Bristol).

MORAL DEBASEMENT PROGRESSIVE

I believe the instances are exceedingly rare of men immediately passing over a clear, marked line of virtue into declared vice and corruption. There are a sort of middle tints and shades between the two extremes; there is something uncertain on the confines of the two empires which they first pass through, and which renders the change easy and imperceptible. There are even a sort of splendid impositions so well contrived, that, at the very time the path of rectitude is quitted for ever, men seem to be advancing into some higher and nobler road of public conduct. Not that such impositions are strong enough in themselves; but a powerful interest, often concealed from those whom it affects, works at the bottom, and secures the operation. Men are thus debauched away from those legitimate connexions, which they had formed on a judgment, early perhaps but sufficiently mature, and wholly unbiased. (*Observations on a Late State of the Nation*).

GOOD MANNERS HELP CORRECT PUBLIC CORRUPTION

Nor is it the worst effect of this unnatural contention, that our *laws* are corrupted. Whilst *manners* remain entire, they will correct the vices of law, and soften it at length to their own temper. But we have to lament, that in most of the late proceedings we see very few traces of that generosity, humanity, and dignity of mind which formerly characterized this nation. War suspends the rules of moral obligation, and what is long suspended is in danger of being totally abrogated. Civil wars strike deepest of all into the manners of the people. They vitiate their politics; they corrupt their morals; they pervert even the natural taste and relish of equity and justice. By teaching us to consider our fellow-citizens in a hostile light, the whole body of our nation becomes gradually less dear to us. The very names of affection and kindred, which were the bond of charity whilst we agreed, become new incentives to hatred and rage when the communion of our country is dissolved. We may flatter ourselves that we shall not fall into this misfortune. But we have no charter of exemption, that I know of, from the ordinary frailties of our nature. (Letter to the Sheriffs of Bristol).

CORRUPTION NOT SELF-REFORMED

Those, who would commit the reformation of India[20] to the destroyers of it, are the enemies to that reformation. They would make a distinction between directors and proprietors, which, in the present state of things, does not, cannot exist. But a right honourable gentleman says, he would keep the present government of India in the court of directors; and would, to curb them, provide salutary regulations;—wonderful! That is, he would appoint the old offenders to correct the old offences; and he

---

20 Burke opposed leaving reform of Indian affairs to the same people whose administration created the mayhem.

would render the vicious and the foolish wise and virtuous, by salutary regulations. He would appoint the wolf as guardian of the sheep; but he has invented a curious muzzle, by which this protecting wolf shall not be able to open his jaws above an inch or two at the utmost. Thus his work is finished. But I tell the right honourable gentleman, that controlled depravity is not innocence; and that it is not the labour of delinquency in chains that will correct abuses. Will these gentlemen of the direction animadvert on the partners of their own guilt? Never did a serious plan of amending any old tyrannical reformers of them. (Speech to the House on Indian Affairs).

THE BRIBED AND THE BRIBERS

If I am to speak my private sentiments, I think that in a thousand cases for one it would be far less mischievous to the public, and full as little dishonourable to themselves, to be polluted with direct bribery, than thus to become a standing auxiliary to the oppression, usury, and peculation, of multitudes, in order to obtain a corrupt support to their power. It is by bribing, not so often by being bribed, that wicked politicians bring ruin on mankind. Avarice is a rival to the pursuits of many. It finds a multitude of checks, and many opposers, in every walk of life. But the objects of ambition are for the few; and every person who aims at indirect profit, and therefore wants other protection, than innocence and law, instead of its rival becomes its instrument. There is a natural allegiance and fealty do you to this domineering, paramount evil, from all the vassal vices, which acknowledge its superiority, and readily militate under its banners; and it is under that discipline alone that avarice is able to spread to any considerable extent, or to render itself a general, public mischief. (Speech to the House).

PROSCRIBING WHOLE GROUPS OF PEOPLE

This way of *proscribing the citizens by denominations and general descriptions,*[21] dignified by the name of reason of state, and security for constitutions and commonwealths, is nothing better at bottom, than the miserable invention of an ungenerous ambition, which would fain hold the sacred trust of power, without any of the virtues or any of the energies that give a title to it: a receipt of policy, made up of a detestable compound of malice, cowardice, and sloth. They would govern men against their will; but in that government they would be discharged from the exercise of vigilance, providence, and fortitude; and therefore, that they may sleep on their watch, they consent to take some one division of the society into partnership of the tyranny over the rest. But let government, in what form it may be, comprehend the whole in its justice, and restrain the suspicious by its vigilance; let it keep watch and ward; let it discover by its sagacity, and punish by its firmness, all delinquency against its power, whenever delinquency exists in the overt acts; and then it will be as safe as ever God and nature intended it should be. Crimes are the acts of individuals, and not of denominations; and therefore arbitrarily to class men under general descriptions, in order to proscribe and punish them in the lump for a presumed delinquency, of which perhaps but a part, perhaps none at all, are guilty, is indeed a compendious method, and saves a world of trouble about proof; but such a method, instead of being law, is an act of unnatural rebellion against the legal dominion of reason and justice; and this vice, in any constitution that entertains it, at one time or other will certainly bring on its ruin. (Speech to the electors of Bristol).

---

21 Burke promoted greater freedoms for suppressed people, especially Catholics and the Irish.

LIBERTY CONNECTED TO VIRTUE

I must fairly tell you, that so far as my principles are concerned, (principles that I hope will only depart with my last breath), I have no idea of a liberty unconnected with honesty and justice. Nor do I believe that any good constitutions of government, or of freedom, can find it necessary for their security to doom any part of the people to a permanent slavery. Such a constitution of freedom, if such can be, is in effect no more than another name for the tyranny of the strongest faction; and factions in republics have been, and are, full as capable as monarchs of the most cruel oppression and injustice. It is but too true, that the love, and even the very idea of genuine liberty is extremely rare. It is but too true, that there are many whose whole scheme of freedom is made up of pride, perverseness, and insolence. They feel themselves in a state of thraldom, they imagine that their souls are cooped and cabined in, unless they have some man, or some body of men, dependent on their mercy. The desire of having some one below them descends to those who are the very lowest of all,—and a Protestant cobbler, debased by his poverty, but exalted by his share of the ruling church, feels a pride in knowing it is by his generosity alone that the peer, whose footman's instep he measures, is able to keep his chaplain from a gaol. (Speech to the Bristol electors).

POLITICS AND THE PULPIT

Supposing, however, that something like moderation were visible in this political sermon; yet politics and the pulpit are terms that have little agreement. No sound ought to be heard in the church but the healing voice of Christian charity. The cause of civil liberty and civil government gains as little as that of religion by this confusion of duties.

Those who quit their proper character to assume what does not belong to them, are, for the greater part, ignorant both of the character they leave, and of the character they assume. Wholly unacquainted with the world in which they are so fond of meddling, and inexperienced in all its affairs, on which they pronounce with so much confidence, they have nothing of politics but the passions they excite. Surely the church is a place where one day's truce ought to be allowed to the dissensions and animosities of mankind. (*Reflection on the Revolution in France*).

AFFECTED PITY FOR THE "POOR"

Let government protect and encourage industry, secure property, repress violence, and discountenance fraud, it is all that they have to do. In other respects, the less they meddle in these affairs the better; the rest is in the hands of our Master and theirs. We are in a constitution of things wherein—"*Modo sol nimius, modo corripit imber.*[22]" But I will push this matter no further. As I have said a good deal upon it at various times during my public service, and have lately written something on it which may yet see the light, I shall content myself now with observing, that the vigorous and laborious class of life has lately got, from the bon ton of the humanity of this day, the name of the "labouring poor." We have heard many plans for the relief of the "labouring poor." This puling jargon is not as innocent as it is foolish. In meddling with great affairs, weakness is never innoxious. Hitherto the name of poor (in the sense in which it is used to excite compassion) has not been used for those who can, but for those who cannot, labour—for the sick and infirm, for orphan infancy, for languishing and decrepit age: but when we affect to pity, as poor, those who must labour, or the world cannot exist, we are trifling with the condition of mankind. It is the common

---

22   Latin, Ovid: One minute the sun's too hot, the next minute a downpour ruins it.

doom of man that he must eat his bread by the sweat of his brow, that is, by the sweat of his body, or the sweat of his mind. If this toil was inflicted as a curse, it is, as might be expected from the curses of the Father of all blessings—it is tempered with many alleviations, many comforts. Every attempt to fly from it, and to refuse the very terms of our existence, becomes much more truly a curse; and heavier pains and penalties fall upon those who would elude the tasks which are put upon them by the great Master Workman of the world, who, in his dealings with his creatures, sympathizes with their weakness, and speaking of a creation wrought by mere will out of nothing, speaks of six days of *labour* and one of *rest*. I do not call a healthy young man, cheerful in his mind, and vigorous in his arms, I cannot call such a man *poor*; I cannot pity my kind as a kind, merely because they are men. This affected pity only tends to dissatisfy them with their condition, and to teach them to seek resources where no resources are to be found, in something else than their own industry, and frugality, and sobriety. Whatever may be the intention (which, because I do not know, I cannot dispute) of those who would discontent mankind by this strange pity, they act towards us, in the consequences, as if they were our worst enemies. (*Letters on a Regicide Peace*).

SELF-INTEREST *ENERGISES*

There must be some impulse besides public spirit to put private interest into motion along with it. Monied men ought to be allowed to set a value on their money; if they did not, there could be no monied men. This desire of accumulation is a principle without which the means of their service to the state could not exist. The love of *lucre*, though sometimes carried to a ridiculous, sometimes to a vicious excess, is the grand cause of prosperity to all states. In this natural, this reasonable, this powerful, this prolific principle, it is for the satirist to expose the ridiculous: it is for the moralist to censure the vicious; it is for the sympathetic heart to reprobate the hard and cruel; it is for the judge to animadvert on the fraud, the extortion, and the oppression; but it is for the statesman to employ it as he finds it, with all its concomitant excellencies, with all its imperfections on its head. It is his part, in this case, as it is in all other cases where he is to make use of the general energies of nature, to take them as he finds them. (*Letters on a Regicide Peace*).

RELIGION STABILISES THE STATE.

I beg leave to speak of our church establishment, which is the first of our prejudices, not a prejudice destitute of reason, but involving in it profound and extensive wisdom. I speak of it first. It is first, and last, and midst in our minds. For, taking ground on that religious system, of which we are now in possession, we continue to act on the early received and uniformly continued sense of mankind. That sense not only, like a wise architect, hath built up the august fabric of states, but like a provident proprietor, to preserve the structure from profanation and ruin, as a sacred temple purged from all the impurities of fraud, and violence, and injustice, and tyranny, hath solemnly and for ever consecrated the commonwealth, and all that officiate in it. This consecration is made, that all who administer in the government of men, in which they stand in the person of God himself, should have high and worthy notions of their function and destination; that their hope should be full of immortality; that they should not look to the paltry pelf[23] of the moment, nor to the temporary and transient praise of the vulgar, but to a solid, permanent existence, in the permanent

---

23 Derogatory term for money.

part of their nature, and to a permanent fame and glory, in the example they leave as a rich inheritance to the world.

Such sublime principles ought to be infused into persons of exalted situations; and religious establishments provided, that may continually revive and enforce them. Every sort of moral, every sort of civil, every sort of politic institution, aiding the rational and natural ties that connect the human understanding and affections to the divine, are not more than necessary, in order to build up that wonderful structure, Man; whose prerogative it is, to be in a great degree a creature of his own making; and who, when made as he ought to be made, is destined to hold no trivial place in the creation. But whenever man is put over men, as the better nature ought ever to preside, in that case more particularly, he should as nearly as possible be approximated to his perfection.

The consecration of the state, by a state religious establishment, is necessary also to operate with a wholesome awe upon free citizens; because in order to secure their freedom, they must enjoy some determinate portion of power. To them therefore a religion connected with the state, and with their duty towards it, becomes even more necessary than in such societies, where the people, by the terms of their subjection, are confined to private sentiments, and the management of their own family concerns. All persons possessing any portion of power ought to be strongly and awfully impressed with an idea that they act in trust; and that they are to account for their conduct in that trust to the one great Master, Author, and Founder of society. This principle ought even to be more strongly impressed upon the minds of those who compose the collective sovereignty, than upon those of single princes. Without instruments, these princes can do nothing. Whoever uses instruments, in finding helps, finds also impediments.

Their power is therefore by no means complete; nor are they safe in extreme abuse. Such persons, however elevated by flattery, arrogance, and self-opinion, must be sensible that whether covered or not by positive law, in some way or other they are accountable even here for the abuse of their trust. If they are not cut off by a rebellion of their people, they may be strangled by the very janissaries[24] kept for their security against all other rebellion. Thus we have seen the king of France sold by his soldiers for an increase of pay. But where popular authority is absolute and unrestrained, the people have an infinitely greater, because a far better founded, confidence in their own power. They are themselves, in a great measure, their own instruments. They are nearer to their objects. Besides, they are less under responsibility to one of the greatest controlling powers on earth, the sense of fame and estimation. The share of infamy, that is likely to fall to the lot of each individual in public acts, is small indeed; the operation of opinion being in the inverse ratio to the number of those who abuse power. Their own approbation of their own acts has to them the appearance of a public judgment in their favour. A perfect democracy is therefore the most shameless thing in the world. As it is the most shameless, it is also the most fearless. No man apprehends in his person that he can be made subject to punishment. Certainly the people at large never ought: for as all punishments are for example towards the conservation of the people at large, the people at large can never become the subject of punishment by any human hand. (*Quicquid multis peccatur inultum*[25].) It is therefore of infinite importance that they should not be suffered to imagine that their will, any more than that of kings, is the standard of right and wrong. They ought to be persuaded that they are full as little entitled, and far less qualified, with safety to themselves, to use

---

24 Elite troops and bodyguards of Ottoman sultans.
25 Latin, from ancient Roman poet Lucan: The sins of the many go unpunished.

any arbitrary power whatsoever; that therefore they are not, under a false show of liberty, but in truth, to exercise an unnatural, inverted domination, tyranically to exact from those who officiate in the state, not an entire devotion to their interest, which is their right, but an abject submission to their occasional will; extinguishing thereby, in all those who serve them, all moral principle, all sense of dignity, all use of judgment, and all consistency of character; whilst by the very same process they give themselves up a proper, a suitable, but a most contemptible prey to the servile ambition of popular sycophants, or courtly flatterers. (*Reflections on the Revolution in France*).

REVERENT LOVE AND RELIGION

True religion has, and must have, a large mixture of salutary fear; and false religions have generally nothing else but fear to support them. Before the Christian religion had, as it were, humanized the idea of the Divinity, and brought it somewhat nearer to us, there was very little said of the love of God. The followers of Plato have something of it, and only something; the other writers of pagan antiquity, whether poets or philosophers, nothing at all. And they who consider with what infinite attention, by what a disregard of every perishable object, through what long habits of piety and contemplation it is that any man is able to attain an entire love and devotion to the Deity, will easily perceive that it is not the first, the most natural and the most striking, effect which proceeds from that idea. (*A Philosophical Enquiry into the Origin of Our Ideas of the Sublime and Beautiful*).

HUMAN FINITITUDE

Whilst we consider the Godhead merely as he is an object of the understanding, which forms a complex idea of power, wisdom, justice, goodness, all stretched to a degree far exceeding the bounds of our comprehension, whilst we consider the Divinity in this refined and abstracted light, the imagination and passions are little or nothing affected. But because we are bound, by the condition of our nature, to ascend to these pure and intellectual ideas, through the medium of sensible images, to judge of these divine qualities by their evident acts and exertions, it becomes extremely hard to disentangle our idea of the cause from the effect by which we are led to know it. Thus, when we contemplate the Deity, his attributes and their operation, coming united on the mind, form a sort of sensible image, and as such are capable of affecting the imagination. Now, though in a just idea of the Deity, perhaps none of his attributes are predominant, yet, to our imagination, his power is by far the most striking. Some reflection, some comparing, is necessary to satisfy us of his wisdom, his justice, and his goodness. To be struck with his power, it is only necessary that we should open our eyes. But whilst we contemplate so vast an object, under the arm, as it were of almighty power, and invested upon every side with omnipresence, we shrink into the minuteness of our own nature, and are, in a manner, annihilated before him. (*A Philosophical Enquiry into the Origin of Our Ideas of the Sublime and Beautiful*).

UNITY IN THE COMMONWEALTH

For that service, for all service, whether of revenue, trade, or empire, my trust is in her interest in the British constitution. My hold of the colonies is in the close affection which grows from common names, from kindred blood, from similar privileges, and equal protection. These are ties, which, though light as air, are as strong as links of iron. Let the colonies always keep the idea of their civil rights associated with your government;—they will cling and grapple to you; and no force under heaven will be of power to tear them from their allegiance. But let it be once understood that your government may be one thing, and their privileges another; that these two things may exist without any mutual relation; the cement is gone; the cohesion is loosened; and everything hastens to decay and dissolution. As long as you have the wisdom to keep the sovereign authority of this country as the sanctuary of liberty, the sacred temple consecrated to our common faith, wherever the chosen race and sons of England worship freedom, they will turn their faces towards you. The more they multiply, the more friends you will have; the more ardently they love liberty, the more perfect will be their obedience. Slavery they can have anywhere. It is a weed that grows in every soil.

They may have it from Spain, they may have it from Prussia. But, until you become lost to all feeling of your true interest and your natural dignity, freedom they can have from none but you. This is the commodity of price, of which you have the monopoly. This is the true act of navigation, which binds to you the commerce of the colonies, and through them secures to you the wealth of the world. Deny them this participation of freedom, and you break that sole bond, which originally made, and must still preserve, the unity of the empire. Do not entertain so weak an imagination, as that your registers and your bonds, your affidavits and your sufferances, your cockets and your clearances, are what form the great securities of your commerce. Do not dream that your letters of office, and your instructions, and your suspending clauses, are the things that hold together the great contexture of this mysterious whole. These things do not make your government. Dead instruments, passive tools as they are, it is the spirit of the English communion that gives all their life and efficacy to them. It is the spirit of the English constitution, which, infused through the mighty mass, pervades, feeds, unites, invigorates, vivifies every part of the empire, even down to the minutest member. (Speech on Conciliation with America).

3

DON'T FOLLOW THE FRENCH REVOLUTIONARIES!

OUR FRENCH DANGERS

In the last age[26] we were in danger of being entangled by the example of France in the net of a relentless despotism. It is not necessary to say anything upon that example. It exists no longer. Our present danger from the example of a people, whose character knows no medium, is, with regard to government, a danger from anarchy; a danger of being led through an admiration of successful fraud and violence, to an imitation of the excesses of an irrational, unprincipled, proscribing, confiscating, plundering, ferocious, bloody, and tyrannical democracy. On the side of religion, the danger of their example is no longer from intolerance, but from atheism; a foul, unnatural vice, foe to all the dignity and consolation of mankind; which seems in France, for a long

---

26   Burke refers to the reign of Louis XIV.

115

time, to have been embodied into a faction, accredited, and almost avowed. (Speech to the House).

THE *NOVELTY* OF FRENCH REVOLUTION

It appears to me as if I were in a great crisis, not of the affairs of France alone, but of all Europe, perhaps of more than Europe. All circumstances taken together, the French revolution is the most astonishing that has hitherto happened in the world. The most wonderful things are brought about in many instances by means the most absurd and ridiculous; in the most ridiculous modes; and, apparently, by the most contemptible instruments. Everything seems out of nature in this strange chaos of levity and ferocity, and of all sorts of crimes jumbled together with all sorts of follies. In viewing this monstrous tragi-comic scene, the most opposite passions necessarily succeed, and sometimes mix with each other in the mind; alternate contempt and indignation; alternate laughter and tears; alternate scorn and horror. (*Reflections on the Revolution in France*).

CAREFUL DISTINCTIONS ARE NEEDED

I certainly have the honour to belong to more clubs than one in which the constitution of this kingdom and the principles of the glorious Revolution[27] are held in high reverence; and I reckon myself among the most forward in my zeal for maintaining that constitution and those principles in their utmost purity and vigour. It is because I do so that I think it necessary for me that there should be no mistake. Those who cultivate the memory of our revolution, and those who are attached

---

27 Burke refers to the Glorious Revolution in England of 1688, which reinforced
Parliament's role and further limited monarchical power.

to the constitution of this kingdom, will take good care how they are involved with persons, who, under the pretext of zeal towards the Revolution and constitution, too frequently wander from their true principles; and are ready on every occasion to depart from the firm but cautious and deliberate spirit which produced the one, and which presides in the other. (*Reflections on the Revolution in France*).

FRENCH AND ENGLISH REVOLUTIONS CONTRASTED

In truth, the circumstances of our revolution (as it is called) and that of France, are just the reverse of each other in almost every particular, and in the whole spirit of the transaction. With us it was the case of a legal monarch attempting arbitrary power—in France it is the case of an arbitrary monarch, beginning, from whatever cause, to legalize his authority. The one was to be resisted, the other was to be managed and directed; but in neither case was the order of the state to be changed, lest government might be ruined, which ought only to be corrected and legalized. With us we got rid of the man, and preserved the constituent parts of the state. There they get rid of the constituent parts of the state, and keep the man. What we did was in truth and substance, and in a constitutional light, a revolution, not made, but prevented. We took solid securities; we settled doubtful questions; we corrected anomalies in our law. In the stable, fundamental parts of our constitution we made no revolution; no, nor any alteration at all. We did not impair the monarchy. Perhaps it might be shown that we strengthened it very considerably. The nation kept the same ranks, the same orders, the same privileges, the same franchises, the same rules for property, the same subordinations, the same order in the law, in the revenue, and in the magistracy; the same lords, the same commons, the same corporations, the same electors.

The church was not impaired. Her estates, her majesty, her splendour, her orders and gradations, continued the same. She was preserved in her full efficiency, and cleared only of a certain intolerance, which was her weakness and disgrace. The church and the state were the same after the revolution that they were before, but better secured in every part.

Was little done because a revolution was not made in the constitution? No! Everything was done; because we commenced with reparation, not with ruin. Accordingly the state flourished. Instead of laying as dead, in a sort of trance, or exposed, as some others, in an epileptic fit, to the pity or derision of the world, for her wild, ridiculous, convulsive movements, impotent to every purpose but that of dashing out her brains against the pavement, Great Britain rose above the standard even of her former self. An era of a more improved domestic prosperity then commenced, and still continues not only unimpaired, but growing, under the wasting hand of time. All the energies of the country were awakened.

England never preserved a firmer countenance, nor a more vigorous arm, to all her enemies, and to all her rivals. Europe under her respired and revived. Everywhere she appeared as the protector, assertor, or avenger, of liberty. A war was made and supported against fortune itself. The treaty of Ryswick[28], which first limited the power of France, was soon after made; the grand alliance very shortly followed, which shook to the foundations the dreadful power which menaced the independence of mankind. The states of Europe lay happy under the shade of a great and free monarchy, which knew how to be great without endangering its own peace at home, or the internal or external peace of any of its neighbours. (Speech to the House).

---

28 This treaty (1697) brought an end to the Nine Years War between France and other European powers, including Great Britain.

THE VALUE OF IMITATING NATURE'S METHOD.

The policy appears to me to be the result of profound reflection; or rather the happy effect of following nature, which is wisdom without reflection, and above it. A spirit of innovation is generally the result of a selfish temper, and confined views. People will not look forward to posterity, who never look backward to their ancestors. Besides, the people of England well know that the idea of inheritance furnishes a sure principle of conservation, and a sure principle of transmission, without at all excluding a principle of improvement. It leaves acquisition free; but it secures what it acquires. Whatever advantages are obtained by a state proceeding on these maxims, are locked fast as in a sort of family settlement; grasped as in a kind of mortmain for ever. By a constitutional policy working after the pattern of nature, we receive, we hold, we transmit our government and our privileges, in the same manner in which we enjoy and transmit our property and our lives. The institutions of policy, the goods of fortune, the gifts of Providence, are handed down to us, and from us, in the same course and order. Our political system is placed in a just correspondence and symmetry with the order of the world, and with the mode of existence decreed to a permanent body composed of transitory parts; wherein, by the disposition of a stupendous wisdom, moulding together the great mysterious incorporation of the human race, the whole, at one time, is never old, or middle-aged, or young, but, in a condition of unchangeable constancy, moves on through the varied tenour of perpetual decay, fall, renovation, and progression. Thus, by preserving the method of nature in the conduct of the state, in what we improve, we are never wholly new; in what we retain, we are never wholly obsolete. By adhering in this manner and on those principles to our forefathers, we are guided not by the superstition of antiquarians, but by the spirit of philosophic analogy. In this choice of inheritance we have given to our frame of polity the image of a relation in blood; binding up the constitution of our country with our dearest domestic ties; adopting our fundamental laws into the bosom of our family affections; keeping inseparable, and cherishing with the warmth of all their combined and mutually reflected charities, our state, our hearths, our sepulchres, and our altars.

Through the same plan of a conformity to nature in our artificial institutions, and by calling in the aid of her unerring and powerful instincts to fortify the fallible and feeble contrivances of our reason, we have derived several other, and those no small benefits, from considering our liberties in the light of an inheritance. Always acting as if in the presence of canonized forefathers, the spirit of freedom, leading in itself to misrule and excess, is tempered with an awful gravity. This idea of a liberal descent inspires us with a sense of habitual native dignity, which prevents that upstart insolence almost inevitably adhering to and disgracing those who are the first acquirers of any distinction. By this means our liberty becomes a noble freedom.

It carries an imposing and majestic aspect. It has a pedigree and illustrating ancestors. It has its bearings and its ensigns armorial. It has its gallery of portraits; its monumental inscriptions; its records, evidences, and titles. We procure reverence to our civil institutions on the principle upon which nature teaches us to revere individual men; on account of their age, and on account of those from whom they are descended. All your sophisters cannot produce anything better adapted to preserve a rational and manly freedom than the course that we have pursued, who have chosen our nature rather than our speculations, our breasts rather than our inventions, for the great conservatories and magazines[29] of our rights and privileges. (*Reflections on the Revolution in France*).

TRIPLE BASIS OF FRENCH REVOLUTION.

Instead of the religion and the law by which they were in a great politic communion with the Christian world, they have constructed their republic on three bases, all fundamentally opposite to those on which the communities of Europe are built. Its foundation is laid in regicide, in Jacobinism, and in atheism; and it has joined to those principles a body of systematic manners, which secures their operation.

If I am asked, how I would be understood in the use of these terms, regicide, Jacobinism, atheism, and a system of corresponding manners, and their establishment? I will tell you:—

I.–REGICIDE.

I call a commonwealth *regicide*, which lays it down as a fixed law of nature, and a fundamental right of man, that all government, not being a democracy, is a usurpation. That all kings, as such, are usurpers; and for being kings may and ought to be put to death, with their wives, families, and adherents. The commonwealth which acts uniformly upon those principles, and which, after abolishing every festival of religion, chooses the most flagrant act of a murderous regicide treason for a feast of eternal commemoration, and which forces all her people to observe it—this I call *regicide by establishment*.

II.–JACOBINISM.

Jacobinism is the revolt of the enterprising talents of a country against

---

29   Gunpowder storage structures.

its property. When private men form themselves into associations for the purpose of destroying the pre-existing laws and institutions of their country; when they secure to themselves an army, by dividing amongst the people of no property the estates of the ancient and lawful proprietors; when a state recognises those acts; when it does not make confiscations for crimes, but makes crimes for confiscations; when it has its principal strength, and all its resources, in such a violation of property; when it stands chiefly upon such a violation, massacring by judgments, or otherwise, those who make any struggle for their old legal government, and their legal, hereditary, or acquired possessions—I call this *Jacobinism by establishment*.

III.–ATHEISM.

I call it *atheism by establishment*, when any state, as such, shall not acknowledge the existence of God as a moral governor of the world; when it shall offer to him no religious or moral worship;–when it shall abolish the Christian religion by a regular decree;–when it shall persecute with a cold, unrelenting, steady cruelty, by every mode of confiscation, imprisonment, exile, and death, all its ministers;–when it shall generally shut up or pull down churches; when the few buildings which remain of this kind shall be opened only for the purpose of making a profane apotheosis of monsters, whose vices and crimes have no parallel amongst men, and whom all other men consider as objects of general detestation, and the severest animadversion of law. When, in the place of that religion of social benevolence, and of individual self-denial, in mockery of all religion, they institute impious, blasphemous, indecent theatric rites, in honour of their vitiated, perverted reason, and erect altars to the personification of their own corrupted and bloody republic;–when schools and seminaries are founded at the public expense to poison mankind, from generation to generation, with the horrible maxims of this impiety;—when wearied out with incessant martyrdom, and the cries of a people hungering and thirsting for religion, they permit it only as a tolerated evil—I call this *atheism by establishment*. (*Letters on a Regicide Peace*).

WHEN GOVERNMENT DESTROYS GOOD MANNERS.

When to these establishments of regicide, of Jacobinism, and of atheism, you add the *correspondent system of manners*, no doubt can be left on the mind of a thinking man concerning their determined hostility to the human race. Manners are of more importance than laws. Upon them, in a great measure, the laws depend. The law touches us but here and there, and now and then. Manners are what vex or soothe, corrupt or purify, exalt or debase, barbarize or refine us, by a constant, steady, uniform, insensible operation, like that of the air we breathe in. They give their whole form and colour to our lives. According to their quality, they aid morals, they supply them, or they totally destroy them. Of this the new French legislators were aware; therefore, with the same method, and under the same authority, they settled a system of manners, the most licentious, prostitute, and abandoned that ever has been known, and at the same time the most coarse, rude, savage, and ferocious. Nothing in the Revolution, no, not to a phrase or gesture, not to the fashion of a hat or a shoe, was left to accident. All has been the result of design; all has been matter of institution. No mechanical means could be devised in favour of this incredible system of wickedness and vice, that has not been employed. The noblest passions, the love of glory, the love of country, have been debauched into means of its preservation and its propagation. All sorts of shows and exhibitions, calculated to inflame and vitiate the imagination, and pervert the moral sense, have been contrived. They have sometimes brought forth five or six hundred drunken women, calling at the bar of the Assembly for the blood of their own children, as being royalists or constitutionalists. Sometimes they have got a body of wretches, calling themselves fathers, to demand the murder of their sons, boasting that Rome had but one Brutus, but that they could show five hundred. There were instances in which they inverted, and retaliated the impiety, and produced sons, who called for the execution of their parents. The foundation of their republic is laid in moral paradoxes. Their patriotism is always prodigy. All those instances to be found in history, whether real or fabulous, of a doubtful public spirit, at which morality is perplexed, reason is staggered, and from which affrighted nature recoils, are their chosen, and almost sole examples for the instruction of their youth.

The whole drift of their institution is contrary to that of the wise legislators of all countries, who aimed at improving instincts into morals, and at grafting the virtues on the stock of the natural affections. They, on the contrary, have omitted no pains to eradicate every benevolent and noble propensity in the mind of men. In their culture it is a rule always to graft virtues on vices. They think everything unworthy of the name of public virtue, unless it indicates violence on the private. All their new institutions (and with them everything is new) strike at the root of our social nature. Other legislators, knowing that marriage is the origin of all relations, and consequently the first element of all duties, have endeavoured, by every art, to make it sacred. The Christian religion, by confining it to the pairs, and by rendering that relation indissoluble, has by these two things done more towards the peace, happiness, settlement, and civilization of the world, than by any other part in this whole scheme of Divine Wisdom. The direct contrary course has been taken in the synagogue of antichrist, I mean in that forge and manufactury of all evil, the sect which predominated in the Constituent Assembly of 1789. Those monsters employed the same, or greater industry, to desecrate and degrade that state, which other legislators have used to render it holy and honourable. (*Letters on a Regicide Peace*).

FRANCE GAVE POWER TO SELF-CENTRED MEN.

Who could flatter himself that these men, suddenly, and, as it were, by enchantment, snatched from the humblest rank of subordination, would not be intoxicated with their unprepared greatness? Who could conceive, that men who are habitually meddling, daring, subtle, active, of litigious dispositions and unquiet minds[30], could easily fall back into their old condition of obscure contention, and laborious, low, unproductive chicane? Who could doubt that, at any expense of the state, of which they understood nothing, they must pursue their private interests, which they understood but too well? It was not an event depending on chance or contingency. It was inevitable; it was necessary; it was planted in the nature of things. They must *join* (if their capacity did not permit them to *lead*) in any project which could procure for them a litigious constitution; which could lay open to them those innumerable lucrative jobs which follow in the train of all great convulsions and revolutions in the state, and particularly all great and violent permutations of property, whose existence had always depended upon whatever render property questionable, ambiguous and insecure? Their objects would be enlarged with their elevation, but their disposition and habits, and mode of accomplishing their designs, must remain the same. (*Reflections on the Revolution in France*).

---

30   Burke refers to the many lawyers among the revolutionaries.

NATIONAL SELF-DESTRUCTION

The French have proved themselves the ablest architects of ruin that ever existed in the world. In one summer they have done their business for us as rivals in a way more destructive than twenty Ramillies or Blenheims[31]. In this very short space of time they have completely pulled down to the ground their monarchy: their church; their nobility; their law; their revenue; their army; their navy; their commerce; their arts; and their manufactures. They now are lying in a sort of trance—an epileptic fit—exposed to the pity or derision of mankind, in wild ridiculous convulsive movements, impotent to every purpose but that of dashing out their brains against the pavement. Yet they are so very unwise as to glory in a revolution which is a shame and disgrace to them. They have made their way to the very worst constitution in the world by the destruction of their country. They were in possession of a good constitution on the very first day when the States met in separate orders. Had they been either virtuous or wise their business then was to secure the stability and independence of the state according to those orders under the monarch on the throne and afterwards to redress grievances. Instead of this they first destroyed all the balances and counterpoises which serve to fix a state and give it a steady direction, and then they melted down the whole into one incongruous mass of mob and democracy. And when they had done this with a perfidy most unexampled and atrocious, they laid the Axe to the root of all property of all national prosperity by confiscating the possessions of the church. They next proceeded systematically to destroy every hold of authority civil or religious on the minds of the people by making and recording a sort of institute or digest of Anarchy called the rights of man, in such a pedantic abuse of elementary principles as would

---

31 Battles at Blenheim (1704) and Ramillies (1706) were English victories over Louis XIV's French forces.

disgrace the imbecility of schoolboys. But the worst effect of all their proceedings is on their military—rendering them fit instruments of every infamous purpose without even the chance of any check or control. Not converting soldiers into citizens but into base hireling mutineers—mercenary sordid deserters wholly destitute of any one honourable principle. Their conduct is one of the fruits of that anarchic spirit from the evils of which even democracy itself is received and cherished by those who are most averse from that *form* as a cure. This army is not an army in corps and with discipline embodied under the respectable patriotic citizens of the state: Nothing like it. No, it is the case of common soldiers' deserting from their officers to join the banditti of a furious and unbridled populace. It is a desertion to a cause the real object of which is hostility not to servitude but to society—levelling all those institutions—breaking all those connections, natural and civil, that regulate and hold together communities by one chain of subordination: raising soldiers against their officers: servants against their masters: tradesmen against their customers: artificers against their employers: tenants against their landlords: curates against their bishops and children against their parents. How would You, Mr Speaker, and how would any of You, Gentlemen, like to have your mansions pulled down and pillaged—your title deeds brought out and burnt before Your faces—your persons abused insulted and destroyed—and your families driven to seek refuge in every corner of Europe—and all this without any fault of yours or any other reason than this—that you were *born gentlemen* and men of property—and were suspected of a desire to preserve your estates and your consideration. Sir, this desertion of the French military was to aid the most execrable, the most detestable sedition the very open professed abominable principle of which is an implacable hostility to *nobility and gentry*. Their savage war whoop is *"A l'Aristocrat"* and by this senseless bloody cry they animate one another to rapine and to murder: while abetted by ambitious men of another class they are crushing all that is virtuous or respectable in the nation and to the utmost of their power dishonouring and disgracing every name by which we formerly knew that there was such a country in the world as France. (Speech to the House).

LIBERTY WITHOUT VIRTUE IS DESTRUCTIVE

Compute your gains: see what is got by those extravagant and presumptuous speculations which have taught your leaders to despise all their predecessors, and all their contemporaries, and even to despise themselves, until the moment in which they became truly despicable. By following those false lights France has brought undignified calamities at a higher price than any nation has purchased the most unequivocal blessings! France has brought poverty by crime! France has not sacrificed her virtue to her interest; but she has abandoned her interest, that she might prostitute her virtue. All other nations have begun the fabric of a new government, or the reformation of an old, by establishing originally, or by enforcing with greater exactness some rites or other of religion. All other people have laid the foundations of civil freedom in severer manners, and a system of more austere and masculine morality. France, when she let loose the reins of regal authority, doubled the license, of a ferocious dissoluteness in manners, and of an insolent religion in opinions and practices; and has extended through all ranks of life, as if she was communicating some privilege, or laying open some secluded benefit, all the unhappy corruptions that usually were the disease of wealth and power. This is one of the new principles of equality in France...

This is unnatural. The rest is in order. They have found their punishment in their success. Laws overturned; tribunals subverted;

industry without vigour; commerce expiring; the revenue unpaid, yet the people impoverished; a church pillaged, and a state not relieved; civil and military anarchy made the constitution of the kingdom; every thing human and divine sacrificed to the idol of public credit, and national bankruptcy the consequence; and to crown it all, the paper securities[32] of new, precarious, tottering power, the discredited paper securities of impoverished fraud, and beggared rapine, held out as a currency for the support of an empire, in lieu of the two great recognized species[33] that represent the lasting conventional credit of mankind, which disappeared and hid themselves in the earth from whence they came, when the principle of property, whose creatures and representatives they were, was systematically subverted.

Were all these dreadful things necessary? Were they the inevitable results of the desperate struggle of determined patriots, compelled to wade through blood and tumult, to the quiet shore of a tranquil and prosperous liberty? No! Nothing like it. The fresh ruins of France, which shock our feelings wherever we can turn our eyes, are not the devastation of a civil war; they are the sad but instructive monument of rash and ignorant counsel in a time of profound peace. (*Reflections on the Revolution in France*).

---

32 Burke refers to *Assignats*, paper money issued by the revolutionary Constituent Assembly. *Assignats* were supposedly backed by the value of the land taken from the French crown and plundered from the Church. Widely printed to deal with the government's debt crisis, and widely forged, the value of *assignats* plummeted.

33 Gold and silver.

NATURAL AND CIVIL RIGHTS.

Far am I from denying in theory, full as far as is my heart from withholding in practice (if I were of power to give or to withhold), the *real* rights of men. In denying their false claims of right, I do not mean to injure those which are real, and are such as their pretended rights would totally destroy. If civil society be made for the advantage of man, all the advantages for which it is made become his right. It is an institution of beneficence; and law itself is only beneficence acting by a rule. Men have a right to live by that rule; they have a right to do justice, as between their fellows, whether their fellows are in politic function, or in ordinary occupation. They have a right to the fruits of their industry, and to the means of making their industry fruitful. They have a right to the acquisitions of their parents; to the nourishment and improvement of their offspring; to instruction in life, and to consolation in death. Whatever each man can separately do, without trespassing upon others, he has a right to do for himself; and he has a right to a fair portion of all which society, with all its combinations of skill and force, can do in his favour. In this partnership all men have equal rights; but not to equal things. He that has but five shillings in the partnership, has as good a right to it, as he that has five hundred pounds has to his larger proportion. But he has not a right to an equal dividend in the product of the joint-stock; and as to the share of power, authority, and direction which each individual ought to have in the management of the state, that I must deny to be amongst the direct original rights of man in civil society; for I have in my contemplation the civil social man, and no other. It is a thing to be settled by convention. If civil society be the offspring of convention, that convention must be its law. That convention must limit and modify all the descriptions of constitution which are formed under it. Every sort of legislature, judicial, or executory power, are its creatures.

They can have no being in any other state of things; and how can any man claim, under the conventions of civil society, rights which do not so much as suppose its existence? Rights which are absolutely repugnant to it? One of the first motives to civil society, and which becomes one of its fundamental rules, is, *that no man should be judge in his own cause.* By this each person has at once divested himself of the first fundamental right of uncovenanted man, that is, to judge for himself, and to assert his own cause. He abdicates all right to be his own governor. He inclusively, in a great measure, abandons the right of self-defence, the first law of nature. Men cannot enjoy the rights of an uncivil and of a civil state together. That he may obtain justice, he gives up his right of determining what it is in points the most essential to him. That he may secure some liberty, he makes a surrender in trust of the whole of it. Government is not made in virtue of natural rights, which may and do exist in total independence of it; and exist in much greater clearness, and in a much greater degree of abstract perfection: but their abstract perfection is their practical defect. By having a right to everything they want everything. Government is a contrivance of human wisdom to provide for human *wants.* Men have a right that these wants should be provided for by this wisdom. Among these wants is to be reckoned the want, out of civil society, of a sufficient restraint upon their passions. Society requires not only that the passions of individuals should be subjected, but that even in the mass and body, as well as in the individuals, the inclinations of men should frequently be thwarted, their will controlled, and their passions brought into subjection. This can only be done *by a power out of themselves,* and not, in the exercise of its function, subject to that will and to those passions which it is its office to bridle and subdue. In this sense the restraints on men, as well as their liberties, are to be reckoned among their rights. But as the liberties and the restrictions vary with times and circumstances, and admit of infinite modifications, they cannot be settled upon any abstract rule; and nothing is so foolish as to discuss them upon that principle.

The moment you abate anything from the full rights of men, each to govern himself, and suffer any artificial, positive limitation upon those rights, from that moment the whole organization of government becomes a consideration of convenience. This it is which makes the constitution of a state, and the due distribution of its powers, a matter of the most delicate and complicated skill. It requires a deep knowledge of human nature and human necessities, and of the things which facilitate or obstruct the various ends, which are to be pursued by the mechanism of civil institutions. The state is to have recruits to its strength, and remedies to its distempers. What is the use of discussing a man's abstract right to food or medicine? The question is upon the method of procuring and administering them. In that deliberation I shall always advise to call in the aid of the farmer and the physician, rather than the professor of metaphysics. The science of constructing a commonwealth, or renovating it, or reforming it, is, like every other experimental science, not to be taught *a priori*. Nor is it a short experience that can instruct us in that practical science, because the real effects of moral causes are not always immediate; but that which in the first instance is prejudicial may be excellent in its remoter operation; and its excellence may arise even from the ill effects it produces in the beginning. The reverse also happens; and very plausible schemes, with very pleasing commencements, have often shameful and lamentable conclusions. In states there are often some obscure and almost latent causes, things which appear at first view of little moment, on which a very great part of its prosperity or adversity may most essentially depend. The science of government being therefore so practical in itself, and intended for such practical purposes, a matter which requires experience, and even more experience than any person can gain in his whole life, however sagacious and observing he may be, it is with infinite caution that any man ought to venture upon pulling down an edifice, which has answered in any tolerable degree for ages the common purposes of society, or on building it up again, without having models and patterns of approved utility before his eyes.

These metaphysic rights entering into common life, like rays of light which pierce into a dense medium, are, by the laws of nature, refracted from their straight line. Indeed in the gross and complicated mass of human passions and concerns, the primitive rights of men undergo such a variety of refractions and reflections, that it becomes absurd to talk of them as if they continued in the simplicity of their original direction. The nature of man is intricate; the objects of society are of the greatest possible complexity: and therefore no simple disposition or direction of power can be suitable either to man's nature, or to the quality of his affairs. When I hear the simplicity of contrivance aimed at and boasted of in any new political constitutions, I am at no loss to decide that the artificers are grossly ignorant of their trade, or totally negligent of their duty. The simple governments are fundamentally defective, to say no worse of them. If you were to contemplate society in but one point of view, all these simple modes of polity are infinitely captivating. In effect each would answer its single end much more perfectly than the more complex is able to attain all its complex purposes. But it is better that the whole should be imperfectly and anomalously answered, than that, while some parts are provided for with great exactness, others might be totally neglected, or perhaps materially injured, by the over-care of a favourite member.

The pretended rights of these theorists[34] are all extremes: and in

---

34   French revolutionary *philosophes.*

proportion as they are metaphysically true, they are morally and politically false. The rights of men are in a sort of *middle*, incapable of definition, but not impossible to be discerned. The rights of men in governments are their advantages, and these are often in balances between differences of good; in compromises sometimes between good and evil, and sometimes between evil and evil. Political reason is a computing principle, adding, subtracting, multiplying, and dividing, morally and not metaphysically or mathematically, true moral denominations.

By these theorists the right of the people is almost always sophistically confounded with their power. The body of the community, whenever it can come to act, can meet with no effectual resistance; but till power and right are the same, the whole body of them has no right inconsistent with virtue, and the first of all virtues—prudence[35]. (*Reflections on the Revolution in France*).

ABSTRACT THEORY OF HUMAN LIBERTY

I love a manly, moral, regulated liberty as well as any gentleman of that society, be he who he will: and perhaps I have given as good proofs of my attachment to that cause in the whole course of my public conduct. I think I envy liberty as little as they do, to any other nation. But I cannot stand forward, and give praise or blame to anything which relates to human actions, and human concerns, on a simple view of the object, as it stands stripped of every relation, in all the nakedness and solitude of metaphysical abstraction. Circumstances (which with some gentlemen pass for nothing) give in reality to every political principle

---

35 Among the cardinal virtues: Prudence, Fortitude, Justice and Temperance, it's Prudence that provides direction for the other virtues.

its distinguishing colour and discriminating effect. The circumstances are what render every civil and political scheme beneficial or noxious to mankind. Abstractedly speaking, government, as well as liberty, is good; yet could I, in common sense, ago, have felicitated France on her enjoyment of a government (for she then had a government) without inquiry what the nature of that government was, or how it was administered? Can I now congratulate the same nation upon its freedom? Is it because liberty in the abstract may be classed amongst the blessings of mankind that I am seriously to felicitate a madman, who has escaped from the protecting restraint and wholesome darkness of his cell, on his restoration to the enjoyment of light and liberty? Am I to congratulate a highwayman and murderer, who has broken prison, upon the recovery of his natural rights? This would be to act over again the scene of the criminals condemned to the galleys, and their heroic deliverer, the metaphysic knight of the sorrowful countenance. When I see the spirit of liberty in action, I see a strong principle at work; and this, for a while, is all I can possibly know of it. The wild *gas*, the fixed air, is plainly broke loose: but we ought to suspend our judgment until the first effervescence is a little subsided, till the liquor is cleared, and until we see something deeper than the agitation of a troubled and frothy surface. I must be tolerably sure, before I venture publicly to congratulate men upon a blessing, that they have really received one. Flattery corrupts both the receiver and the giver; and adulation is not of more service to the people than to kings.

I should therefore suspend my congratulations on the new liberty of France, until I was informed how it had been combined with government; with public force; with the discipline and obedience of armies; with the collection of an effective and well-distributed revenue; with morality and religion; with solidity and property; with peace and order; with civil and social manners. All these (in their way) are good things too; and, without them, liberty is not a benefit whilst it lasts, and is not likely to continue long. The effect of liberty to individuals, is, that they may do what they please: we ought to see what it will please them to do before we risk congratulations, which may be soon turned into complaints. Prudence would dictate this in the case of separate, insulated, private men; but liberty, when men act in bodies, is *power*. Considerate people, before they declare themselves, will observe the use which is made of *power*; and particularly of so trying a thing as *new* power in *new* persons, of whose principles, tempers, and dispositions, they have little or no experience, and in situations where those who appear the most stirring in the scene may possibly not be the real movers. (*Reflections on the Revolution in France*).

DANGER OF ABSTRACT VIEWS

It is not worth our while to discuss, like sophisters, whether, in no case, some evil, for the sake of some benefit, is to be tolerated. Nothing universal can be rationally affirmed on any moral or any political subject. Pure metaphysical abstraction does not belong to these matters. The lines of morality are not like ideal lines of mathematics. They are broad and deep as well as long. They admit of exceptions; they demand modifications. These exceptions and modifications are not made by the process of logic, but by the rules of prudence. Prudence is not only the first in rank of the virtues political and moral, but she is the director, the regulator, the standard of them all. Metaphysics cannot live without definition; but prudence is cautious how she defines. Our courts cannot be more fearful in suffering fictitious cases to be brought before them for eliciting their determination on a point of law, than prudent moralists are in putting extreme and hazardous cases of conscience upon emergencies not existing. Without attempting therefore to define, what never can be defined, the case of a revolution in government, this, I think, may be safely affirmed, that a sore and pressing evil is to be removed, and that a good, great in its amount, and unequivocal in its nature, must be probable almost to certainty, before the inestimable price of our own morals, and the well-being of a number of our fellow-citizens, is paid for a revolution. If ever we ought to be economists even to parsimony, it is in the voluntary production of evil. Every revolution contains in it something of evil. (*An Appeal from the New to the Old Whigs*).

HATING VICES, BUT NOT LOVING PEOPLE

What your [French revolutionary] politicians thinks the marks of a bold, hardy genius, are only proofs of a deplorable want of ability. By their violent haste, and their defiance of the process of nature, they are delivered over blindly to every projector and adventurer, to every alchemist and empiric. They despair of turning to account any thing that is common. Diet is nothing in their system of remedy. The worst of it is, that this their despair of curing common distempers by regular methods, arises not only from a defect of comprehension but, I fear, from some malignancy of disposition. Your legislators seem to have taken their opinions of all professions, ranks and offices, from the declamations and buffooneries of satirists; who would themselves be astonished if they were held to the letter of their own descriptions. By listening only to these your leaders regard all things only on the side of their vices and faults, and view these vices and faults under every colour of exaggeration. It is undoubtedly true, though it may seem paradoxical; but in general, those who are habitually employed in finding and displaying faults, are unqualified for the work of reformation: because their minds are not only unfurnished with patterns of the fair and good, but by habit they come to take no delight in the contemplation of those things. By hating vices too much, they come to love men too little. It is therefore not wonderful, that they should be indisposed and unable to serve them. From hence arises the complexional disposition of some of your guides to pull every thing in pieces. (*Reflections on the Revolution in France*).

POLITICAL LAZYNESS

I am convinced that there are men of considerable talent among the popular leaders of the National Assembly. Some of them display eloquence in their speeches and their writings. This cannot be without powerful and cultivated talents. But eloquence may exist without a proportionable degree of wisdom. When I speak of ability, I am obliged to distinguish. What they have done towards the support of their system bespeaks no ordinary men. In the system itself, taken as the scheme of a republic constructed for procuring the prosperity and security of the citizen, and for promoting the strength and grandeur of the state, I confess myself unable to find anything which displays, in a single instance, the work of a comprehensive and disposing mind, or even the provisions of a vulgar prudence. Their purpose everywhere seems to have been to evade and slip aside from difficulty. This it has been the glory of the great masters in all the arts to confront and to overcome; and when they had overcome the first difficulty, to turn it into an instrument for new conquests over new difficulties; thus to enable them to extend the empire of their science; and even to push forward, beyond the reach of their original thoughts, the landmarks of the human understanding itself. Difficulty is a severe instructor, set over us by the supreme ordinance of a parental guardian and legislator, who knows us better than we know ourselves, and loves us better too. *Pater ipse colendi haud facilem esse viam voluit*[36]. He that wrestles with us strengthens our nerves, and sharpens our skill. Our antagonist is our helper. This amicable conflict with difficulty obliges us to an intimate acquaintance with our object, and compels us to consider it in all its relations. It will not suffer us to be superficial. It is the want of nerves or understanding for such a task, it is the degenerate fondness for tricking short-cuts, and little fallacious facilities, that has in so many parts of the world created governments with arbitrary powers. They have created the late arbitrary monarchy of France. They have created the arbitrary republic of Paris. With them defects in wisdom are to be supplied by the plenitude of force. They get nothing by it. Commencing their labours on a principle of sloth, they have the common fortune of slothful men. The difficulties, which they rather had eluded than escaped, meet them again in their course; they multiply and thicken on them; they are involved, through a labyrinth of confused detail, in an industry without limit, and without direction; and, in conclusion, the whole of their work becomes feeble, vicious, and insecure.

It is this inability to wrestle with difficulty which has obliged the arbitrary assembly of France to commence their schemes of reform with abolition and total destruction. But is it in destroying and pulling down that skill is displayed? Your mob can do this at least as well as your assemblies. The shallowest understanding, the rudest hand, is more than equal to the task. Rage and frenzy will pull down more in half and hour than prudence, deliberation, and foresight can build up in a hundred years. The errors and defects of the old establishments are visible and palpable. It calls for little ability to point them out; and, where absolute power is given, it requires but a word wholly to abolish

---

36 *Georgics,* Virgil: "The father of agriculture himself willed that the way should not be easy..."

the vice and the establishment together. The same lazy but restless disposition, which loves sloth but hates quiet, directs these politicians when they come to work for supplying the place of what they have destroyed. To make everything the reverse of what they have seen is quite as easy as to destroy. No difficulties occur in what has never been tried. Criticism is almost baffled in discovering the defects of what has not existed; and eager enthusiasm and cheating hope have all the wide field of imagination in which they may expatiate with little or no opposition.

At once to preserve and to reform is quite another thing. (*Reflections on the Revolution In France*).

MILITANT ATHEISM AND INSTABILITY

The most cruel and horrid blow that can be offered to civil society is through atheism. Do not promote diversity; when you have it, bear it; have as many sorts of religion as you find in your country; there is a reasonable worship in all of them. The others, the infidels, are outlaws of the constitution, not of this country, but of the human race. They are never, never to be supported, never to be tolerated. Under the systematic attacks of these people I see some of the props of good government already begin to fail; I see propagated principles which will not leave to religion even a toleration. I see myself sinking every day under the attacks of these wretched people—how shall I arm myself against them? By uniting all those in affection who are united in the belief of the great principles of the Godhead that made and sustains the world. They who hold revelation give double assurance to the country. Even the man who does not hold relevation, yet who wishes that it were proved to him, who observes a pious silence with regard to it, such a man, though not a Christian, is governed by religious principles. Let him be tolerated in this country. Let it be a serious religion, natural or revealed, take what you can get; cherish, blow up the slightest spark. One day it may be a pure and holy flame. By this proceeding you form an alliance, offensive and defensive, against those great ministers of darkness in the world who are endeavouring to shake all the works of God established in order and beauty. (Speech for the Relief of the Protestant Dissenters).

ATHEIST BIGOTRY

The literary cabal had some years ago formed something like a regular plan for the destruction of the Christian religion. This object they pursued with a degree of zeal which hitherto had been discovered only in the propagators of some system of piety. They were possessed with a spirit of proselytism in the most fanatical degree; and from thence, by an easy progress, with the spirit of persecution according to their means. What was not to be done towards their great end by any direct or immediate act, might be wrought by a longer process through the medium of opinion. To command that opinion, the first step is to establish a dominion over those who direct it. They contrived to possess themselves, with great method and perseverance, of all the avenues to literary fame. Many of them indeed stood high in the ranks of literature and science. The world had done them justice; and in favour of general talents forgave the evil tendency of their peculiar principles. This was true liberality; which they returned by endeavouring to confine the reputation of sense, learning, and taste to themselves or their followers. I will venture to say that this narrow, exclusive spirit has not been less prejudicial to literature and to taste, than to morals and true philosophy. Those atheistical fathers have a bigotry of their own; and they have learnt to talk against monks with the spirit of a monk. But in some things they are men of the world. The resources of intrigue are called in to supply the defects of argument and wit. To this system of literary monopoly was joined an unremitting industry to blacken and discredit in every way, and by every means, all those who did not hold to their faction. To those who have observed the spirit of their conduct, it has long been clear that nothing was wanted but the power of carrying the intolerance of the tongue and of the pen into a persecution which would strike at property, liberty, and life.

The desultory and faint persecution carried on against them, more from compliance with form and decency, than with serious resentment, neither weakened their strength, nor relaxed their efforts. The issue of the whole was, that, what with opposition, and what with success, a violent and malignant zeal, of a kind hitherto unknown in the world, had taken an entire possession of their minds, and rendered their whole conversation, which otherwise would have been pleasing and instructive, perfectly disgusting. A spirit of cabal, intrigue, and proselytism, pervaded all their thoughts, words, and actions. And, as controversial zeal soon turns its thoughts on force, they began to insinuate themselves into a correspondence with foreign princes; in hopes, through their authority, which at first they flattered, they might bring about the changes they had in view. To them it was indifferent whether these changes were to be accomplished by the thunderbolt of despotism, or by the earthquake of popular commotion. The correspondence between this cabal and the late king of Prussia, will throw no small light upon the spirit of all their proceedings. For the same purpose for which they intrigued with princes, they cultivated, in a distinguished manner, the monied interest of France; and partly through the means furnished by those whose peculiar offices gave them the most extensive and certain means of communication, they carefully occupied all the avenues to opinion.

Writers, especially when they act in a body, and with one direction, have great influence on the public mind; the alliance, therefore, of these writers with the monied interest, had no small effect in removing the popular odium and envy which attended that species of wealth. These writers, like the propagators of all novelties, pretended to a great zeal for the poor, and the lower orders, whilst in their satires they rendered hateful, by every exaggeration, the faults of courts, of nobility, and of priesthood. They became a sort of demagogues. They served as a link to unite, in favour of one object, obnoxious wealth to restless and desperate poverty. (*Reflections on the Revolution in France*).

ZIG-ZAGGING POLITICIANS COMBINING WITH ATHEISTS.

In the revolution of France two sorts of men were principally concerned in giving a character and determination to its pursuits: the philosophers and the politicians. They took different ways, but they met in the same end. The philosophers had one predominant object, which they pursued with a fanatical fury; that is, the utter extirpation of religion. To that every question of empire was subordinate. They had rather domineer in a parish of atheists than rule over a Christian world. Their temporal ambition was wholly subservient to their proselytizing spirit, in which they were not exceeded by Mahomet himself. They who have made but superficial studies in the natural history of the human mind, have been taught to look on religious opinions as the only cause of enthusiastic zeal and sectarian propagation. But there is no doctrine whatever, on which men can warm, that is not capable of the very same effect. The social nature of man impels him to propagate his principles, as much as physical impulses urge him to propagate his kind. The passions give zeal and vehemence. The understanding bestows design and system. The whole man moves under the discipline of his opinions. Religion is among the most powerful causes of enthusiasm. When anything concerning it becomes an object of much meditation, it cannot be indifferent to the mind. They who do not love religion, hate it. The rebels to God perfectly abhor the author of their being. They hate him "with all their heart, with all their mind, with all their soul, and with all their strength." He never presents himself to their thoughts, but to menace and alarm them. They cannot strike the sun out of heaven, but they are able to raise a smouldering smoke that obscures him from their own eyes. Not being able to revenge themselves on God, they have a delight in vicariously defacing, degrading, torturing, and tearing in pieces his image in man. Let no one judge of them by what he has conceived of them, when they were not incorporated, and had no lead. They were then only passengers in a common vehicle. They were then carried along with the general motion of religion in the community, and, without being aware of it, partook of its influence. In that situation, at worst, their nature was left free to counter-work their principles. They despaired of giving any very general currency to their opinions. They considered them as a reserved privilege for the chosen few. But when the possibility of dominion, lead, and propagation, presented itself, and that the ambition, which before had so often made them hypocrites, might rather gain than lose by a daring avowal of their sentiments, then the nature of this infernal spirit, which has "evil for its good," appeared in its full perfection.

Nothing indeed but the possession of some power can with any certainty discover what at the bottom is the true character of any man. Without reading the speeches of Vergniaud, Francian of Nantes, Isnard,[37] and some others of that sort, it would not be easy to conceive the passion, rancour, and malice of their tongues and hearts. They worked themselves up to a perfect frenzy against religion and all its professors. They tore the reputation of the clergy to pieces by their infuriated declamations and invectives, before they lacerated their bodies by their massacres. This fanatical atheism left out, we omit the principal feature in the French revolution, and a principal consideration with regard to the effects to be expected from a peace with it.

The other sort of men were the politicians. To them, who had little or not at all reflected on the subject, religion was in itself no object of love or hatred. They disbelieved it, and that was all. Neutral with regard to that object, they took the side which in the present state of things might best answer their purposes. They soon found that they could not do without the philosophers; and the philosophers soon made them sensible that the destruction of religion[38] was to supply them with means of conquest, first at home, and then abroad. The philosophers were the active internal agitators, and supplied the spirit and principles: the second gave the practical direction. Sometimes the one predominated in the composition, sometimes the other. The only difference between them was in the necessity of concealing the general design for a time, and in their dealing with foreign nations; the fanatics going straightforward and openly, the politicians by the surer mode of zigzag. In the course of events, this, among other causes, produced fierce and bloody contentions between them. But at the bottom they thoroughly agreed in all the objects of ambition and irreligion, and substantially in all the means of promoting these ends. (*Letters on a Regicide Peace*).

---

37   Prominent members of French revolutionary factions.

38   To raise funds, the revolutionaries confiscated church property and placed it for sale.

MISANTHROPIC ATHEISTS.

These philosophers are fanatics; independent of any interest, which if it operated alone would make them much more tractable, they are carried with such a headlong rage towards every desperate trial, that they would sacrifice the whole human race to the slightest of their experiments. I am better able to enter into the character of this description of men than the noble duke can be. I have lived long and variously in the world. Without any considerable pretensions to literature in myself, I have aspired to the love of letters. I have lived for a great many years in habitudes with those who professed them. I can form a tolerable estimate of what is likely to happen from a character chiefly dependent for fame and fortune on knowledge and talent, as well in its morbid and perverted state as in that which is sound and natural. Naturally, men so formed and finished are the first gifts of Providence to the world. But when they have once thrown off the fear of God, which was in all ages too often the case, and the fear of men, which is now the case, and when in that state they come to understand one another, and to act in corps, a more dreadful calamity cannot arise out of hell to scourge mankind.

Nothing can be conceived more hard than the heart of a thorough-bred metaphysician. It comes nearer to the cold malignity of a wicked spirit than to the frailty and passion of a man. It is like that of the principle of evil himself, incorporeal, pure, unmixed, dephlegmated, defecated evil. It is no easy operation to eradicate humanity from the human breast. What Shakespeare calls "the compunctious visitings of nature[39]," will sometimes knock at their hearts, and protest against their murderous speculations. But they have a means of compounding with their nature. Their humanity is not dissolved. They only give

---

39 *Macbeth.*

it a long prorogation. They are ready to declare, that they do not think two thousand years too long a period for the good that they pursue. It is remarkable, that they never see any way to their projected good but by the road of some evil. Their imagination is not fatigued with the contemplation of human suffering through the wild waste of centuries added to centuries of misery and desolation. Their humanity is at their horizon—and, like the horizon, it always flies before them. The geometricians and the chemists bring the one from the dry bones of their diagrams, and the other from the soot of their furnaces, dispositions that make them worse than indifferent about those feelings and habitudes which are the supports of the moral world.

Ambition is come upon them suddenly; they are intoxicated with it, and it has rendered them fearless of the danger which may from thence arise to others or to themselves. These philosophers consider men in their experiments no more than they do mice in an air-pump, or in a recipient of mephitic gas. Whatever his grace may think of himself, they look upon him, and everything that belongs to him, with no more regard than they do upon the whiskers of that little long-tailed animal, that has been long the game of the grave, demure, insidious, spring-nailed, velvet-pawed, green-eyed philosophers, whether going upon two legs or upon four. (*Further Reflections on the Revolution in France*).

AN *UN*DISCIPLINED MILITARY

With them [the French revolutionaries] the question was not between despotism and liberty. The sacrifice they made of the peace and power of their country was not made on the altar of freedom. Freedom, and a better security for freedom than that they have taken, they might have had without any sacrifice at all. They brought themselves into all the calamities they suffer, not that through them they might obtain a British Constitution; they plunged themselves headlong into those calamities, to prevent themselves from settling into that Constitution, or into any thing resembling it.

The worst effect of all their proceeding was on their military, which was rendered an army for every purpose but that of defence. It was not an army in corps and with discipline, and embodied under the respectable patriot citizens of the State in resisting tyranny. Nothing like it. It was the case of common soldiers deserting from their officers, to join a furious, licentious populace. It was a desertion to a cause, the real object of which was to level all those institutions, and to break all those connections, natural and civil, that regulate and hold together the community by a chain of subordination; to raise soldiers against their officers; servants against their masters; tradesmen against their customers; artificers against their employers; tenants against their landlords; curates against their bishops; and children against their parents. That this cause of theirs was not an enemy to servitude, but to society.

He knew too well, and he felt as much as any man, how difficult it was to accommodate a standing army to a free constitution, or to any constitution. An armed, disciplined, body is, in its essence, dangerous to liberty; undisciplined, it is ruinous to society. Its component parts are, in the latter case, neither good citizens nor good soldiers. What have they thought of in France, under such a difficulty as almost puts the human faculties to a stand? They have put their army under such a variety of principles of duty, that it is more likely to breed litigants, pettifoggers, and mutineers, than soldiers. They have set up, to balance their crown army, another army, deriving under another authority, called a municipal army—a balance of armies, not of orders. These latter they have destroyed with every mark of insult and oppression. States may, and they will best, exist with a partition of civil powers. Armies cannot exist under a divided command. This state of things he thought, in effect, a state of war, or, at best, but a truce instead of peace, in the country. (Speech to the House on events in France).

CONDITIONS RIPE FOR A *COUP D'ETAT*.

It is besides to be considered whether an assembly like yours, even supposing that it was in possession of another sort of organ through which its orders were to pass, is fit for promoting the obedience and discipline of an army. It is known that armies have hitherto yielded a very precarious and uncertain obedience to any senate, or popular authority; and they will least of all yield it to an assembly which is only to have the continuance of two years. The officers must totally lose the characteristic of military men is they see with perfect submission and due admiration the dominion of pleaders; who military policy, and the genius of those who command (if they should have any), must be as uncertain as their duration is transient. In the weakness of one kind of authority, and the fluctuation of all, the officers of an army will remain for some time mutinous and full of faction, until some popular general, who understands the art of conciliating the soldiery, and who possesses the true spirit of command, shall draw the eyes of all men upon himself. Armies will obey him on his personal account. There is no other way of securing military obedience in this state of things. But the moment in which that event shall happen, the person who really commands the army is your master; the master (that is little) of your king; the master of your assembly; the master of your whole republic. (*Reflections on the Revolution in France*).

DESPOTISM

It is the nature of despotism to abhor power held by any means but its own momentary pleasure; and to annihilate all intermediate situations between boundless strength on its own part, and total debility on the part of the people. (*Thoughts on the Cause of the Present Discontents*).

The strong struggle in every individual to preserve possession of what he has found to belong to him and to distinguish him, is one of the securities against injustice and despotism implanted in our natures. (*Reflections on the Revolution in France*).

Justice is itself the great standing policy of civil society; and any departure from it, under any circumstances, lies under the suspicion of being no policy at all.

When men are encouraged to go into a certain mode of life by the existing laws, and protected in that mode as in a lawful occupation—when they have accommodated all their ideas, and all their habits to it—when the law had long made their adherence to its rules a ground of reputation, and their departure from them a ground of disgrace and even of penalty—I am sure it is unjust in legislature, by an arbitrary act, to offer a sudden violence to their minds and feelings; forcibly to degrade them from their state and condition, and to stigmatize with shame and infamy that character and those customs which before had made the measure of their happiness and honour. If to this is to be added an expulsion from their habitations, and a confiscation of all their goods, I am not sagacious enough to discover how this despotic sport, made of the feelings, consciences, prejudices, and properties of men, can be discriminated from the rankest tyranny.

I hope we shall never be so totally lost to all sense of the duties imposed upon us by the law of social union, as, upon any pretext of public service, to confiscate the goods of a single unoffending citizen. Who but a tyrant (a name expressive of everything which can vitiate and degrade human nature) could think of seizing on the property of men, unaccused, unheard, untried, by whole descriptions, by hundreds and thousands together? Who that had not lost every trace of humanity could think of casting down men of exalted rank and sacred function, some of them of an age to call at once for reverence and compassion, of casting them down from the highest situation in the commonwealth, wherein they were maintained by their own landed property, to a state of indigence, depression and contempt? (*Reflections on the Revolution in France*).

OUT OF PARLIAMENT: A RETROSPECTIVE

Gentlemen, I have had my day[40]. I can never sufficiently express my gratitude to you for having set up me in a place wherein I could lend the slightest help to great and laudable designs. If I have had my share in any measure giving quiet to private property and private conscience; if by my vote I have aided in securing to families the best possession, peace; if I have joined in reconciling kings with their subjects, and subjects to their prince; if I have assisted to loosen the foreign holdings of the citizen, and taught him to look for his protection to the laws of his country, and for his comfort to the good-will of his countrymen;—if I have taken my part with the best of men in the best of their actions, I can shut the book;—I might wish to read a page or two more—but this is enough for my measure. I have not lived in vain.

Gentlemen, the melancholy event of yesterday reads to us an awful

---

40 Burke lost his Bristol seat in 1780 to another candidate, Mr. Coombs. The seat of Malton was found for Burke and he resumed his political career for 14 more years, but this speech is a fair summary of his aims.

lesson about being too much troubled by any of the objects of ordinary ambition. The worthy gentleman who has snatched from us at the moment of election, and in the middle of the contest, whilst his desires were as warm, and his hopes as eager as ours, has feelingly told us what shadows we are, and what shadows we pursue...I humbly and respectfully take my leave of the sheriffs, the candidates, and the electors, wishing heartily that the choice may be for the best, at a time which calls, if ever a time did call, for service that is not nominal. It is no plaything you are about. (Speech after the *lost* Bristol election.)

FURTHER READING

Camus, Albert. *The Rebel.* New York: Knopf Doubleday Publishing Group [reissue], 1999.

Chesterton, G.K. *The Outline of Sanity.* Norfolk, VA.: HIS Press, 2001.

Eliot, T.S. *Christianity & Culture: The Idea of a Christian Society and Notes Towards the Definition of Culture.* Orlando, Fl.: Harcourt, 1960.

Fenwick, Peter. *The Fragility of Freedom: Why Subsidiarity Matters.* Brisbane: Connor Court, 2014.

Fenwick, Peter. *The Fortunate: Ten Great Writers Highlight How We Created Free and Affluent Societies.* Brisbane: Connor Court, 2022.

Furnell, Gary. *The Hardest Path is the Easiest: Exploring the Wisdom Literature with Pascal, Burke, Kierkegaard and Chesterton.* Brisbane: Connor Court, 2021.

Gray, John. *Seven Types of Atheism.* New York: Macmillan, 2018.

Haval, Vaclav. *The Power of the Powerless.* London: Vintage Classics, 2018.

James, Clive. *Cultural Amnesia: Notes on the Margin of My Time.* London: Picador, 2007.

Kierkegaard, Soren. *Works of Love.* Translated by Howard and Edna Hong. New York: Harper Perennial Modern Thought, 2009

Maritain, Jacques. *Man and the State. Chicago:* University of Chicago Press, 1951.

Pope Benedict XVI. *Caritas in veritae [On Integral Human Development in Charity and Truth]*, 2009.

Pope John Paul II. *Centesimus annus: On the Hundredth Anniversary of Rerum Novarum.* 1991.

Pope John Paul II. *Memory and Identity: Personal Reflections.* London: Weidenfeld & Nicolson, 2005.

Pope John Paul II. *Sollicitudo Rei Socialis [On Social Concerns]*, 1988.

Schumacher, E.F. *Small is Beautiful: a Study of Economics as if People Mattered.* London: Abacus, 1974.

Scruton, Roger. *Fools, Frauds and Firebrands: Thinkers of the New Left.* London: Bloomsbury Continuum, 2016.

Scruton Roger. *How to be a Conservative.* London: Bloomsbury Continuum, 2014.

Scruton, Roger. *The Uses of Pessimism: and the Danger of False Hope.* Oxford: Oxford University Press, 2013.

Solzhenitsyn, Aleksandr. *The Gulag Archipelago: an Experiment in Literary Investigation.* Abridged, with a foreword by Jordan B. Peterson. London: Vintage, 2018.

www.ingramcontent.com/pod-product-compliance
Lightning Source LLC
Chambersburg PA
CBHW051109030726
47504CB00006B/1866